1|5

With Hemingway

With Hemingway

A Year in Key West and Cuba

ARNOLD SAMUELSON

Random House New York

Grateful acknowledgment is made to *Esquire* magazine for permission to reprint
excerpts from the October 1935, October 1961 and May 1981 issues of *Esquire*.

All photographs are from the collection of the author.

Library of Congress Cataloging in Publication Data
Samuelson, Arnold, 1912–1981.
With Hemingway.
1. Hemingway, Ernest, 1899–1961—Biography.
2. Novelists, American—20th century—Biography.
I. Title.
PS3515.E37Z795   1984   813'.52 [B]   84-42632
ISBN 0-394-53983-4

Manufactured in the United States of America
98765432
First Edition

To Jim Lovett, a maestro in essence

Foreword by Diane Darby

"Writers writing about writers are about as
interesting as painters would be if they painted
painters."

—ERNEST HEMINGWAY TO THE MAESTRO

IN THE SPRING of 1934, Arnold Samuelson hitchhiked from Minnesota down to Key West to meet Ernest Hemingway in hopes that
he might spare him a few minutes to talk about writing. He ended
up spending almost an entire year with the writer, his family and
his guests in Key West, Cuba and the Gulf Stream. He was the
inspiration for Hemingway's "Monologue to the Maestro," a piece
published in *Esquire* the following year that offered humorous, yet
valuable, advice to young writers. And, for reasons strange as any
fiction, Arnold Samuelson, my father, became Hemingway's only
acknowledged protégé.

After he passed away in 1981, I fell heir to a cache of timeworn,
faded Hemingway memorabilia consisting of letters, photographs
and a ship's log dictated to my father by Hemingway during the
quiet intervals while they fished. He also left behind a three-hun-
dred-page manuscript in which he outlined their conversations and
described events while they were fresh in his mind. The manuscript
was written almost entirely during his stay, in part with Hemingway's assistance. Over the years, he had crossed out large sections
of it, added a sentence here and there and developed alternate begin-
nings, but it was never edited for publication. With the sole exception of his epilogue in *Esquire* after Hemingway's death, my father
kept his feelings about Ernest Hemingway to himself.

I was in a quandary trying to decide what, if anything, I should
do with the material when I came across James Walcott's review
of *Ernest Hemingway's Selected Letters* in the May 1981 issue of
Esquire.

. . . the book represents perhaps the last big bang of the Hemingway
industry, the last log to be kindled in his honor. Along with Hemingway's
own memoir, *A Moveable Feast* . . . there have been volumes of reminis-

cences from a brother, a wife, friends, rivals, casual bystanders and disgruntled spear-carriers . . . If stags could talk, they would dictate memoirs describing the tremulous moment Hemingway's bullet grazed their antlers.

Nineteen thirty-four was the year Hemingway wrote about kuduslaying in *Green Hills of Africa,* acquired the *Pilar,* helped reclassify marlin in the North Atlantic and tried to harpoon a sperm whale—events which, while interesting and not widely chronicled, nevertheless fell into the "if stags could talk" category.

Only after reading most of what Hemingway had written, and most of what had been written about him, did I determine there was, in fact, room for my father's memoir. What I found unique about it was its deceptive simplicity. This is what it was like to talk and write and fish with Ernest Hemingway as seen through the eyes of a twenty-two-year-old Midwestern farm boy. Hemingway's brother, Leicester, seemed to capture their relationship with these words:

> Ernest was never very content with life unless he had a spiritual kid brother nearby. He needed someone he could show off to as well as teach. He needed uncritical admiration. If the kid brother could show a little worshipful awe, that was a distinct aid in the relationship. I made a good kid brother when I was around but I couldn't be around regularly.

I whipped the manuscript into shape in much the same way my father was taught to whip big fish: by giving myself plenty of slack, striking some parts and pumping up others, reeling all the while, and finally mastering it. Why the author never worked it over himself is a matter of conjecture. What *is* known is that he did not want his experience lost to posterity, especially if it could help other aspiring writers.

An unexpected revelation was discovering so many similarities between the two men. There is no doubt that Hemingway had a powerful influence on my father. He always dressed in Hemingway fashion, with his belt outside the loops; for an original touch he carved his sandals out of old tires. While Hemingway had his cats, my father was comforted by a large pack of dogs, of which Blackie was the ringleader. And, in later years, his gray beard gave him the "Papa" look. These affectations, if that is what they were, were easy enough to understand. Hemingway had been imitated before!

Similarities beyond the power of his influence, so hard to understand and difficult to explain, are brought out here because the life of my father, before and after Ernest Hemingway, can best be told in these terms.

Arnold Samuelson was born on February 6, 1912, in a sod house in North Dakota, the son of Norwegian immigrant wheat farmers. He spent much of his childhood riding horseback in the coulees, fishing, reading and avoiding farm labor. He wanted to be a writer all his life; his mother wanted him to become a minister.

I was particularly struck by the similarity of their family relationships. Without going into great detail, both men had mothers who were unconventional for their day in that they avoided cooking and housekeeping; their husbands baked and helped with meal preparation. Both mothers fulfilled their own needs and encouraged their children to become achievers. The two Samuelson sisters became teachers and my father's brother became a medical doctor. My father himself majored in journalism at the University of Minnesota, although he never officially graduated because he wouldn't pay the $5 diploma fee.

At the age of nineteen, both men sustained a psychological shock that conditioned their view of life. With Hemingway, it was the near fatal wound he received in Italy during World War I. With my father, it was the brutal murder in 1932 of his favorite sister by Winnie Ruth Judd, which became infamous as the trunk murder case.

Both men grew up to be six feet tall, well built, with masculine good looks and big hands and feet; both took up boxing as a hobby. They worked as cub reporters; Hemingway on the Kansas City *Star* and my father on the Minneapolis *Tribune*.

Jobs were scarce in the Depression, and in 1932 my father set out in a November snowstorm with a companion to see the world. He carried shears to trade haircuts for meals along the way, played the violin in makeshift orchestras and relied on hitchhiking for transportation. He furnished the Sunday *Tribune* with a series of "Wandering Boy" articles and awaited spring in a log cabin in Northern California. Here he speared salmon with a pitchfork, decorated his Christmas tree with cigarette butts and became a devotee of Ernest Hemingway. The following year he bummed down to Key West, riding the rails into a city where eighty percent of the population was destitute or on relief. He had nothing to live on but a

crushed loaf of bread and no place to stay but the bull pen of the
city jail. For almost anyone else, meeting Ernest Hemingway would
have been anticlimactic. This is where the book begins, and we
have a shared year in the life of two writers, a time in which everything they did was in some way connected to writing.

When my father left Key West, he returned to Minneapolis, published another article about Gulf Stream fishing in *Outdoor Life*
and built houses for his brother. In 1937, he sold his first fiction,
"Mexico for Tramps," to *Esquire;* was congratulated by his mentor
and married the woman he had been courting for five years. They
took off on the back of an Indian 4 motorcycle for a honeymoon
tour of the North American continent; he wrote by the campfire
while his new bride stalked wild game with a .22 rifle. He broke
wild broncs for ranchers and retrained spoiled polo ponies for Fred
Roe in Texas, helped his brother build a hospital in Minneapolis
and worked on a government construction project near the Arctic
Circle during World War II.

In 1945, he and his wife moved to Texas and lived a Thoreau-
style existence next to the Colorado River on the outskirts of a
small town named Robert Lee. The secluded home, ever phoneless,
was surrounded by seven acres of mesquite trees, cactus plants,
rattlesnakes and roadrunners. They had two children, Eric and
me, operated a lumber company, built prefabricated houses and
owned rental property.

My father kept a journal and wrote constantly, but he was never
satisfied with his efforts. In 1955, he sold another story to *Esquire*,
"One Too Many," and Hemingway sent him a telegram saying "HAP-
PIEST YOUR SALE ESQUIRE. VERY PROUD. SURE YOU'LL SELL OTHERS IF
STORIES AS GOOD AS YOUR LETTERS. BEST LUCK. ERNEST."

Most of his writing during those years took the form of letters
to the editor. A self-taught lawyer and political gadfly, he was not
averse to taking a position on public issues, usually the unpopular
one. After he retired, he took a greater interest in music and his
writing became sporadic. He devoted the rest of his life to "self-
inflicted music lessons," restoring old violins and "letting the rest
of the world muddle through in the various quaint ways it muddles."

My most potent childhood memory was seeing Fellini's *La Strada*,
with Anthony Quinn as the strong man who followed the circus
around in his own trailer and who could break out of heavy metal
chains but not out of the shell of loneliness that kept him from

reaching the people he loved. I recognized my father on the screen and I think, now, I may have been watching Hemingway, too. Learning Anthony Quinn hopes to play the role of Ernest Hemingway on Broadway was particularly significant for me.

The lives of Hemingway and my father were marked by a pattern of exhilaration and depression, a pattern that intensified as they grew older. This account takes place while both men were their true selves, buoyant and self-possessed, before all the rigors of life took their toll. From what Hemingway's intimates say, and from what I know about my father, both men were authentically fearless, boundlessly generous and had enormous charisma. They could learn anything with amazing speed, and never lost the quality of adolescent enthusiasm. Both of them exhibited the same contradictory behavior, had an ambivalent attitude toward women and could be mercurial with friends. Using words for weapons, they could be cruel and bullying. Not to everyone, but to many.

Neither suffered fools, phonies, intellectuals, politicians or a litany of others lightly. The shared trait I found most obvious was what a critic called Hemingway's "one grave fault": his "sadistic facetiousness." The gravity of this fault would seem to depend on how close one comes to the receiving end. Few people ever came closer than my father in "Monologue to the Maestro," but he was delighted with the recognition when Hemingway wrote in October 1935:

> He was an excellent night watchman and worked hard on the boat and at his writing but at sea he was a calamity; slow where he should be agile, seeming sometimes to have four feet instead of two feet and two hands, nervous under excitement, and with an incurable tendency toward sea-sickness and a peasant reluctance to take orders. Yet he was always willing and hard working if given plenty of time to work in.
>
> We called him the Maestro because he played the violin, this name was eventually shortened to the Mice, and a big breeze would so effectually slow up his co-ordination that your correspondent once remarked to him, "Mice, you certainly must be going to be a hell of a good writer because you certainly aren't worth a damn at anything else."
>
> On the other hand his writing improved steadily. He may yet be a writer. But your correspondent, who sometimes has an evil temper, is never going to ship another hand who is an aspirant writer; nor go through another summer off the Cuban or any other coast accompanied by questions and answers on the practice of letters. If any more aspirant writers come on board the Pilar let them be females, let them be very beautiful, and let them bring champagne.

When Hemingway died, President Kennedy issued a statement saying ". . . he almost single handedly transformed the literature and the ways of thought of men and women in every country of the world." Ernest Hemingway was a spiritually powerful writer with an important message for the twentieth century. To the degree this book furthers interest in his writing and his message, our mission, my father's and mine, is fulfilled.

Contents

CONTENTS

With Hemingway

1

Hemingway

IN THE SPRING of 1934, I hitchhiked from Minneapolis down to Key West to meet Ernest Hemingway. I was not invited. I had read one of his short stories, "One Trip Across," which later became the first part of *To Have and Have Not.* That story gave me the impulse to travel two thousand miles to meet the writer. At best I hoped he might spare me a few minutes to talk about writing.

It seemed a damn fool thing to do, but a twenty-two-year-old tramp during the Great Depression didn't have to have much reason for what he did. I was headed south at a time when the other bums were following the birds north. At least my wild-goose chase had a destination. Most of the other bums were just getting the hell out of the last town and heading toward easier pickings.

There seemed a good chance E. H. would show at his house in Key West. He was back from a hunting trip in Africa. I had seen a newspaper picture of his arrival on the boat in New York with his wife. That was all I had to go on.

I caught the last freight train leaving the Florida mainland for Key West. It was headed south over the long bridges between the keys and finally right out over the ocean. It couldn't happen now— the tracks have been torn out—but it happened then, almost as in a dream.

It was a short freight train, with one passenger coach and five sealed boxcars, and the only place to ride was on top. I sat alone on the roof of the middle boxcar with the engine puffing smoke right up ahead and the caboose following close behind. I could feel the wheels pounding the invisible rails somewhere below me and there was ocean water on all sides as far as I could see. Looking down over the side of the car, I saw the sun lighting the clear shallow water.

The train moved with a slow clackety-clack rumble. There was not much breeze and the smoke had time to drift off to one side. I sat on the catwalk with my knapsack beside me thinking this

3

must be the most beautiful train ride ever, and it was absolutely free. It was obvious the trainmen knew I was there, but nobody bothered me.

I was riding the boundary between the Atlantic Ocean and the Gulf of Mexico on a perch forty feet off the water. I saw several fish lying in schools on the ocean floor, idly sunning themselves. Some of them looked four feet long. I wondered if any of them were sharks. Anyway, they paid no attention to overhead freight trains.

After eighty miles, this slow, beautiful train ride over the ocean would come to an end. I could see a patch of land floating on the water up ahead. It looked bigger than the other keys and there were buildings on it, far off but coming closer.

That would be Key West, the end of the line. I had bummed all over the United States and Key West was the first place I had been warned to stay away from.

"Hey, Bub, you're headed the wrong way," a bum had told me at the yard in Homestead. "That train's headed for Key West. There ain't nothing there. When you get there all you can do is turn around and come back. If you can get back. If they find you panhandling in Key West, the cops don't fool with you. They throw your ass in jail. If you head back north on a freight, they pick you off as an illegal immigrant. You might even end up on a chain gang."

I was thinking about this as the train chugged leisurely along and I decided, Hell, this ride is worth going to jail for.

But the Hemingway business seemed more and more stupid the closer I got. What would I say to him? "Hello, how are you?" And what would he say to me? "Scram?" He probably picked a remote place like Key West to stay away from bums like me. If I did get a chance to meet him, I wouldn't have the vaguest idea what to say.

I was a dirty bastard. You get that way riding freights, especially on top where the smoke is. The soot gets all over you and you get train soot on anything you touch. I was in no shape to call on anybody. The first thing I had to do was get cleaned up and change clothes.

Now we were coming to the last of the islands, and there was a little depot off to the left. I swung my knapsack onto my back and climbed down the handrails as the train slowed down, stepping free onto the island that was Key West.

There were no cops in sight and nobody seemed to pay much attention to me. But a man carrying a knapsack on his back was definitely out of place on the island. From here there was no place to hike to.

One of the boxcars would go to Cuba on the Havana Ferry, and the others unloaded in Key West. The engine would turn around, pick up the empties, the passenger coach and the caboose and head back north to the mainland over the same tracks we had come down on.

I got a drink of water at the depot and headed across the tracks. In one of the sheds I met a couple Conchs butchering a giant turtle. I learned that native islanders were named for the conch, a tough little mollusk that lives in the waters off Key West. There were boats with fishermen on board selling fish to the natives. Some kids were doing what I needed to do. They wore cut-off trousers for swimming trunks, and were diving off the dock. They were all below working age.

Nearly all the cigar factories had shut down because of Havana competition. Fishing and shrimping was bad. There was very little to do and the young men were gone to find jobs in the mainland, leaving the young and the old and the women. There were a lot of women. Black and white and beautiful. Many in both colors. There were some men still around, though, and they all knew about Hemingway.

At the turtling dock, a Conch who had chopped open a live turtle with a big chopping ax told me, while resting, "I don't see nothing smarter about that guy Hemingway than anybody else, but they say he is one smart son of a bitch. He don't look it, but he can sit down to a typewriter and come up with a thousand bucks. That's more'n I make in a whole year."

Another Conch said, "By God, I can't figure him out. When he came here just a short time ago, he was broke. He couldn't even afford to rent a little boat to go fishing. I know because I heard him bellyaching about not having money to get out and fish. He was just a hard-up tourist with no money to spend. And now look at what he's got. The biggest house in town, a whole damned bunch of servants and he's just got through spending a hundred thousand bucks on a safari in Africa, and be damned if he didn't take Charles Thompson along as a guest, all expenses paid, and then be damned if they didn't send for Charles's wife to meet them in France, all expenses paid, and now they say he's got the damnedest, fanciest fishing boat that was ever built on its way from New York. And hell, it's not a fishing boat, it's a goddamned yacht from the Wheeler Shipyards, with two motors built to individual specifications. Beats the hell out of me."

"It's just like I said," the first Conch said. "He don't look no smarter than anybody else but he must be one smart son of a bitch. You got to hand it to him."

"And I know for a fact he tipped the carpenters a hundred bucks apiece, over their wages, when they got through building him that office above his garage. Nobody around here ever done that before."

"You sure can't see it on him," said another. "He's never dressed up. Goes around in khakis cut off at the ankles. Belt never in the loops. He never wears shoes. Just bedroom slippers without socks. Ain't nobody here that can figure that guy out. We never seen none like him before and here we get all kinds."

My first home in Key West was the bull pen of the Key West city jail. A night cop found me on the planking of the turtle dock, sleeping on my back to save my hipbones, with my knapsack for a pillow. I had been sleeping very well when he awoke me and invited me to go with him to the jail. I'd have a cot and be much more comfortable, he said, and if some crime were committed, I would not be jailed as a suspect. It was clearly an offer I could not refuse. I went with him because I had about eight dollars and no idea how long it would have to last. It wasn't enough to afford a hotel room. My last job had been in Miami, working as a handyman in a rooming house for ten cents an hour.

What the cop didn't tell me about were the mosquitoes. On the dock there had been a cool breeze off the sea and no mosquitoes. In the jail there was no sea breeze, there were no screens over the open windows and the mosquitoes, big ones, came in through the bars. The hospitality of the Key West city jail was so well known that I was the only tramp in town and I had the jail to myself. There were no other guests or prisoners.

I slept in a hammock with all my clothes on, including my shoes. As a sort of delaying action, I dug out all my extra shirts from my knapsack to cover my face and hands. They got through, but it took them longer, and there were short periods when I could sleep.

I was under arrest every night and released every morning to see if I could find my way out of town. If I was still in town at night, I had to report to the mosquitoes. The cops at the jail said nothing to me when I left in the morning nor when I came back at night. They weren't interested in any conversation but they always seemed surprised each day I stayed.

I fought the mosquitoes at night, got most of my sleep during the day and strolled the town as happy as a first-class tourist, living on nothing but a crushed loaf of bread that was crammed in my knapsack. I went around town asking about Ernest Hemingway. He had gone to the mainland a few days, and was expected back any time—and I was on a great adventure, asking natives about the writer I hoped to meet.

As I strolled around, I found the natives were quite willing to open up and talk about him to a tramp stranger in town. There was one thing they could not discuss, however, and that was his writing. Until I went into the Key West *Citizen Weekly* newspaper office, I found nobody who had read a Hemingway book.

When I knocked on the front door of Ernest Hemingway's house in Key West, he came out and stood squarely in front of me, squinting with annoyance, waiting for me to speak. I had nothing to say. I couldn't recall a word of my prepared speech. He was a big man, tall, narrow-hipped, wide-shouldered, and he stood with his feet spread apart, his arms hanging at his sides. He was crouched forward slightly with his weight on his toes, in the instinctive poise of a fighter ready to hit. He had a heavy jaw and a full black mustache, and his dark eyes, which were almost closed, looked me over the way a boxer measures his opponent for the knockout punch.

It was obvious he needed no bouncer to keep tramps off his property. He could handle that job himself.

"What do you want?" he asked.

"I bummed down from Minneapolis to see you," I said, very ill at ease.

"What about?"

"I just want to visit."

It was going from bad to worse. I could tell it in his eyes. When I said I wanted to visit, he thought I meant to move in and stay indefinitely as a guest. He had just seen Dos Passos off and wanted to be alone to get some writing done, and here comes this young tramp he had never seen or even heard of and says he wants to visit! I was puzzled and thought there must be some misunderstanding that called for an explanation.

"I read your story 'One Trip Across' in *Cosmopolitan,* and I liked it so much I came down to have a talk with you," I said.

"You just want to talk?"

"Yes."

"That's different," he said, relaxing and becoming friendly. "Why the hell didn't you say you just wanted to chew the fat? I thought you wanted to visit."

"No, I just wanted to talk," I said, very happy that everything had cleared up so well.

"I'm busy now. Can you come around tomorrow?"

"Any time."

"Make it one-thirty. I've got some things to do now."

"Thanks. One-thirty, then." I began to walk backward toward the gate.

"Wait. I'll drive you downtown."

"No, that's all right. I can walk."

"I was going down for the mail anyway," he said, falling into step beside me. "Wait a minute. I forgot my keys."

He went in for his keys and we walked around to the car shed in the rear.

"Are you a writer?" he asked.

"Not yet, but I want to be one."

"It's a tough racket."

"It's the only thing I give a damn about, but it's so hard for me to do."

"That doesn't mean anything. It's hard for me, too. Have you had anything published?"

"Some hobo stuff in the newspapers is all. It wasn't the writing that made them take it. I was just the stuff I had."

"The stuff is all that counts in anything. It's the same in fiction."

We backed out of his garage in his Model A Ford roadster and drove down a narrow street past old, unpainted wooden houses, very close together, and leaning palm trees.

"Ever go to college?" E. H. asked.

"I took journalism at the University of Minnesota, but I always got poor grades in English."

"That's a good sign. If they get good grades at college, they're usually imitators. They haven't learned to write their own stuff and chances are they never will. Where do you want me to take you?"

"I'll get off any place downtown."

"Where do you stay? I'll take you anywhere you want to go."

"This will be good right here," I said, when we were on Duval Street. I didn't want to be taken to the city jail.

"How are you fixed for money?" he asked, stopping by the Ideal restaurant.

"I've got plenty."

"If the police question you, tell them you're my friend and you're down for a visit."

"Thanks."

"I'm sorry I was rude."

"That's all right."

"I'm glad to have met you and I'll see you tomorrow, then."

We shook hands and I watched him drive off to the post office. He left me with that damned marvelous feeling you can have only once in a lifetime if you are a young man who wants to become a writer and you have just met the man you admire as the greatest writer alive and you know instinctively he is already your friend.

The next afternoon I took another walk on Whitehead Street toward Hemingway's house. I was in a very different mood that day. The fear and doubts I had had during the two weeks I spent riding the freight trains and hitchhiking from the North, not knowing whether E. H. would refuse to see me when I arrived, were gone. Now he had told me to come at one-thirty, and I was on my way.

It was a warm day in late April. The sun had baked the paint off the small wooden houses that were the dull gray color of naked lumber decaying in the sun and rain. There were a few small children playing on the street outside the Negro church, a few loafers sitting in the shade of the corner grocery store, others under their porch roofs smoking their pipes and listening to the Cuban rumba music on the radio. A middle-aged man passed on a bicycle. There were no automobiles on the street, and it was very quiet.

I walked past several blocks of little old houses built close together and then came to the big open corner yard with a flat lawn, surrounded by a tall iron fence and palm trees. In the center, the Hemingway house was like an old courthouse, built to stand against hurricanes after all the wood shacks had blown away. It was a square, two-story concrete mansion built during the Civil War.

I found E. H. sitting on the porch in the shade, looking very comfortable in his khaki pants and bedroom slippers, with his New York *Times* and a glass of whiskey. Seeing me at the gate, he got up and met me on the sunny side of the house.

"How are you?" he said, shaking my hand. "We'll sit down over here."

E. H. had me join him in the shade of the north porch. From there the outside of the house was as private as a bedroom. You were at his home but not in it. Almost like talking to a man out on the street.

"You've got a fine place here," I said, taking a padded wicker chair beside him on the porch, from where we could see the peacocks dragging their long tails by the iron fence, sticking their heads through the bars and looking for a place to get out.

"Yes, it's not bad," E. H. said.

"That was a swell story you had in *Cosmopolitan.*"

"Yes. It was a good story."

"It was the best story I ever read." It sounded stupid after I said it.

"It was a tough one."

"That was good, where he wondered if the Chink's bite was poisonous and then he decided, what the hell, the Chink maybe scrubbed his teeth three times a day."

"I was at sea ninety days before I could write that story, and it took me six weeks to write it. Have you ever tried to write fiction?"

"Yes. Last winter I wrote sixteen to eighteen hours a day until my head was a vacuum and I'd hit the bed dead tired. I tried damned hard. I wrote two novels and about twenty short stories, but it was all crap and they didn't get any better. I was feeling very depressed and when I read your story in *Cosmopolitan,* I decided to come down and see you."

"The most important thing I've learned about writing is never write too much at a time," Hemingway said, tapping my arm with his finger. "Never pump yourself dry. Leave a little for the next day. The main thing is to know when to stop. Don't wait till you've written yourself out. When you're still going good and you come to an interesting place and you know what's going to happen next, that's the time to stop. Then leave it alone and don't think about it; let your subconscious mind do the work. The next morning, when you've had a good sleep and you're feeling fresh, rewrite what you wrote the day before. When you come to the interesting place and you know what is going to happen next, go on from there and stop at another high point of interest. That way, when you get through, your stuff is full of interesting places and when you write a novel you never get stuck and you make it interesting as you go along. Every day go back to the beginning and rewrite the whole thing and when it gets too long, read at least two or three chapters before you start to write and at least once a week go back to the start. That way you make it one piece. And when you go over it, cut out everything you can. The main thing is to know what to leave out. The way you tell whether you're going good is by what you can throw away. If you can throw away stuff that would make a high point of interest in somebody else's story, you know you're going good."

Hemingway spoke emphatically, as if he had already taken a personal interest in my work and wanted to help me all he could.

"Don't get discouraged because there's a lot of mechanical work to writing. There is, and you can't get out of it. I rewrote the first part of *A Farewell to Arms* at least fifty times. You've got to work it over. The first draft of anything is shit. When you first start to write you get all the kick and the reader gets none, but after you learn to work it's your object to convey everything to the reader so that he remembers it not as a story he had read but something that happened to himself. That's the true test of writing. When you can do that, the reader gets the kick and you don't get any. You just get hard work and the better you write the harder it is because every story has to be better than the last one. It's the hardest work there is. I like to do and can do many things better than I can write, but when I don't write I feel like shit. I've got the talent and I feel that I'm wasting it."

I listened carefully, trying to remember everything he said and not lose any of it, because when the interview was over I thought I would never see him again.

"Another thing," he said. "You can't write what you don't know about. Anything purely imaginary is poetry. You've got to absolutely know your place and your people or your story will take place in a vacuum. Then you invent as you go along. When you stop working for the day you know what is going to happen next but you don't know what will happen after that, and you don't know how it will end until you're through."

"Do you mean to say you write a story without having any plot to start off with?"

"The best ones are written that way. If you know a good story, go ahead and write it. That's the kind you write at one sitting, but the best ones are made up as you go along from day to day. They're a hell of a lot harder to write but it's more interesting for you and it's more interesting to the reader. If you don't know how a story is going to turn out how can the reader tell?

"Another thing is, never compete with living writers. You don't know whether they're good or not. Compete with the dead ones you know are good. Then when you can pass them up you know you're going good. You should have read all the good stuff so that you know what has been done, because if you have a story like one somebody else has written, yours isn't any good unless you can write a better one. In any art you're allowed to steal anything if you can make it better, but the tendency should always be upward instead of down. And don't ever imitate anybody. All style is, is the awkwardness of a writer in stating a fact. If you have a way of your own, you are fortunate, but if you try to write like somebody else, you'll have the awkwardnesses of the other writer as well as your own. What writers do you like to read?"

"I liked Stevenson's *Kidnapped* and *Walden Pond* by Thoreau. I can't think of the others off hand."

"Ever read *War and Peace?*"

"No."

"That's a damned good book. You ought to read it. We'll go up to my workshop and I'll make out a list you ought to read."

His workshop was over the garage in back of the house. I followed him up an outside stairway into his workshop, a square room with a tile floor and shuttered windows on three sides and long shelves of books below the windows to the floor. In one corner was a big antique flat-topped desk and an antique chair with a high back. E. H. took the chair in the corner and we sat facing each other across the desk. He found a pen and began writing on a piece of paper and during the silence I was very ill at ease. I realized I was taking up his time, and I wished I could entertain him with my hobo experiences but thought they would be too dull and kept my mouth shut. I was there to take everything he would give and had nothing to return.

"It's hard for me to tell, but you seem to be serious," E. H. said at last. "Seriousness is one thing you've got to have. Big-time writing is the most serious business there is, and imaginative writing is the peak of the art. Another thing you've got to have is talent. Some people never can write fiction. What would you do if you found out you couldn't write fiction?"

"I don't know. How can a man know if he's got talent?"

"You can't. Sometimes you can go on writing for years before it shows. If a man's got it in him, it will come out sometime. The only thing I can advise you is to keep on writing but it's a damned tough racket. The only reason I make any money at it is I'm a sort of literary pirate. Out of every ten stories I write, only one is any good and I throw the other nine away. The editors want my stuff and I've got them in a position where they bid for it and I play off one against the other until they pay for the one as if they had bought all ten. It makes them jealous and they'd like nothing better than to see me come down. When you start to write everybody is wishing you luck, but when you're going good, they try to kill you. The only way you can ever stay on top is by writing good stuff."

"How about imagination?" I asked. "What if a man can't invent?"

"You learn to invent when you keep on writing."

"Even if you can't do anything at the start?"

"Sometimes."

"There was something else I wanted to ask you. I like to live alone a lot. I can't stand to be around people all the time and I wondered if that was bad for a writer."

"No. That makes you more sensitive to people when you do see them. When I left for Africa last fall, I was so damned disgusted with the human race I never wanted to see anybody again. Remember, it's not who you are but what you do that counts. With the possible exception of your mother, nobody gives a damn if you live or die. As an individual you are nothing. Nobody cares what happens to you. You have got to get into the heads of other people."

"Last year I spent a few months hitchhiking and riding freights in the West. Do you think bumming around is good experience for a writer?"

"Yes. I'd like to do it, but I'm tied up here with my wife and family. You want to watch yourself, though, so you don't get to be moving all the time. You ought to stay in one place long enough to learn something about it. You should be able to pick up some good stuff in those lousy transient camps. Have you ever read *Huckleberry Finn?*"

"A long time ago."

"You ought to read it again. It's the best book an American ever wrote, up to the place where Huck finds the nigger after he's been stolen. It marks the beginning of American literature. Ever read 'The Blue Hotel' by Stephen Crane"?

"No."

"Here's a list of books any writer should have read as a part of his education," he said, handing me the following list:

Stephen Crane—
  The Blue Hotel
  The Open Boat.

—

Madame Bovary—Gustave Flaubert.)
Dubliners—James Joyce—
The Red and the Black—By Stendhal—2
(Of Human Bondage—Somerset Maugham)—
Anna Karenina—Tolstoy—3
War and Peace—Tolstoy—4
Buddenbrooks—Thomas Mann—5—
Hail and Farewell—George Moore—
Brothers Karamazoff—Doestoevsky—6
Oxford Book of English Verse—
The Enormous Room—E. E. Cummings.
Wuthering Heights—Emily Bronte
Far Away and Long Ago—W. H. Hudson—
The American—Henry James.

Ernest Hemingway.

"If you haven't read these, you just aren't educated. They represent different types of writing. Some may bore you, others might inspire you and others are so beautifully written they'll make you feel it's hopeless for you to try to write. I think I've got 'The Blue Hotel' here. Have you read *A Farewell to Arms?*"

"No, I haven't."

"I felt good when I finished that. I knew I'd left them something to shoot at." He went over to the shelves and drew out two books and handed them to me. One was a collection of short stories by Stephen Crane and the other *A Farewell to Arms*. "I wish you'd

Stephen Crane –
    The Blue Hotel
    The Open Boat.
Madame Bovary – Gustave Flaubert)
Dubliners – James Joyce –
The Red and the Black – By Stendhal – 2
(Of Human Bondage – Somerset Maugham) –

Anna Karenina – Tolstoy – 3
War and Peace – Tolstoy – 4
Buddenbrooks – Thomas Mann – 5
Hail and Farewell – George Moore –
• Brothers Karamazoff – Dostoevsky – 6.
Oxford Book of English Verse –
The Enormous Room – E. E. Cummings.
Wuthering Heights – Emily Brontë
Far Away and Long Ago – W. H. Hudson –
The American – Henry James.

Ernest Hemingway

send it back when you get through with it. It's the only one
I have of that edition."

"I'll bring them back tomorrow. Thanks."

"What do you intend to do now?"

"I'd like to get a boat out to Cuba, but they say it can't be done
so I suppose I'll have to go back up North."

"Do you speak Spanish?"

"No."

"Then you wouldn't get much out of Cuba. Ever been to sea?"

"No."

"That makes it tough. They only want men who are already broken in. I'm going to Cuba this summer, but on a boat that size,
where there's a limited amount of space, everybody on board has
to be able to do his share of the work. If only one man in the
crew did the wrong thing, he might wreck the ship, so I couldn't
very well take an inexperienced man along."

I nodded.

"If you had experience at sea, it would be different," he said.

"That's what they all tell me. I tried to get out on every port
on the West Coast and they all said the same thing. I had to have
experience. I don't know how a man is going to get it."

"It's pretty hard to break in."

Hemingway stood up and I thought he wanted me to leave.

"Well, thanks. I sure appreciate what you told me about writing,"
I said. "I'll bring the books back. You must find me pretty dull
company, so I'd better go."

"No, it isn't that. I've got some work to do. If you think of any
more questions you'd like to ask about writing, come around tomorrow afternoon. I hope you have good luck with your writing."

"Thanks. Same to you."

I took the books back to the city jail. I did not feel like staying there another night, and the next afternoon I finished reading
A Farewell to Arms, intending to catch the first freight out for Miami. At one o'clock, I brought the books back to Hemingway's
house.

Pauline Hemingway came to the door wearing slacks, with her
black hair brushed back in a boy's haircut. She was built like a
boy and wore no makeup. Her face was tanned from being out in
the sun and there was nothing you could see she had been doing
to make herself beautiful except keeping her weight down.

"I think Ernest wants to see you," she said. "Would you mind waiting? He'll be back in a little while. Have a seat."

Wondering what he could possibly want to see me about, I waited on the porch until his car drew up and stopped at the gate and he came in carrying a bunch of letters and two New York newspapers.

"How are you?" he said.

"Pretty good. I brought your books back."

"There is something I want to talk to you about. Let's sit down," he said thoughtfully. "After you left yesterday, I was thinking I'll need somebody to sleep on board my boat. What are you planning on now?"

"I haven't any plans."

"I've got a boat being shipped from New York. I'll have to go up to Miami Tuesday and run her down and then I'll have to have someone on board. There wouldn't be much work. If you want the job, you could keep her cleaned up in the mornings and still have time for your writing."

"That would be swell."

"There wouldn't be much money in it but it would be good experience. You'd be fishing with us every day we go out. You'd learn how to fish and you'd be serving a sort of seaman's apprenticeship so it would be easier for you to get another job when you leave."

"Swell."

"Of course, I don't know you very well, but you seem to be the sort of person that can be trusted. Do you drink?"

"Not much. Just a little moonshine when I was a kid."

"That's good. The owner is the only person who can get drunk on board a boat." Ernest then hollered at his boy, Louis, to bring us a couple of whiskies. As we drank them, celebrating the fact that I was not a drunk, Ernest asked, "How much wages do you want?"

"I'd leave that up to you."

"No, you'll have to say how much you want."

"Anything is all right with me. I know you can get men for practically nothing in the South."

"No, that isn't true. I'm not very flush right now, but it would be worth a dollar a day for me to have someone I can trust on the boat."

"I'd gladly do it for nothing."

"No. It's worth a dollar a day. Then this summer, if you get over being seasick and learn how to fish, and if you want to go, I might take you along to Cuba as a guest."

I couldn't believe it.

"In Cuba, I'll pick up a crew to take care of the boat and about all you'd have to do would be to hold out the second rod. If you get a strike from something big that looks like a record fish, I'll take over the rod, but you'll get a bellyful of fishing. If you need money over there, I'd pay you wages."

"No, I wouldn't need the money."

"Of course, you can't tell yet how you'll take to the sea. Some people never get used to it."

"I hope nothing happens so I can't go," I said, already worrying about it.

"That's a long way off yet. I think Pauline has something she would like to have you do. You told me yesterday you had worked as a carpenter. Are you good at making cupboards?"

"I've only done rough work but if she'll show me what she wants, I'll try."

"We'd better get your stuff first. I can fix you up with a place to sleep here till the boat comes."

"I'll walk down and get it."

"I'll drive you down. Where have you got your stuff?"

"In the city jail."

"I'll drive you down," he said.

The cops at the jail seemed to think nothing of it that I should move from their mosquito chamber to the home of Ernest Hemingway. They saw his Model A roadster outside waiting for me. They saw me come out of it. They saw Ernest at the wheel waiting and they never said a word.

Back at the big house, I threw my knapsack into the garage, where I was fixed up with a cot. There were no extra rooms in the house. When guests came to Key West to visit, they stayed at a hotel.

Ernest advanced me ten dollars on future wages and Pauline told the cook to fix me something to eat. It came out on a tray, a good meal served with a glass of tomato juice. I was eating again. It was my first meal since Miami.

As soon as I finished the meal, Pauline put me to work. She showed me how she wanted the cupboard built under the kitchen sink and I promised to do my best. I began working on it that afternoon, and was very anxious to make a good impression so that E. H. would not change his mind about taking me to Cuba. I could not believe that I would go with him but I thought there might be a chance if I was very careful. The disadvantage about my first job was that I was not really a carpenter.

The kitchen cabinet was falling to pieces and needed new shelves and new doors. I had to use warped lumber from a shed that had been torn down, and the only tools I could find were a hammer and a dull saw and a rusted plane. The cupboard had to be fitted to the floor which, being very old, had uneven boards sagged out of square with the walls. I worked hard and made a lot of noise. It took me several days to complete a job that should have been done in a few hours.

The hammering and pounding and sawing in the kitchen did not harmonize with the clatter of dishpans. Isabelle, the very much colored and overweight cook, started calling things goddamned sons of a bitches, and it became obvious to Pauline that it was not enough that I stay out of her road while she was preparing a meal. It was necessary that I get out of the kitchen altogether and stay out till it was safe to go back in. So I had quite a bit of free time to look around while Isabelle was cooking.

It was during this time that Sullivan the boilermaker was called in to fix the cistern pump and I was sworn to secrecy. Sully, a successful mechanic who had his own shop downtown, told me never to tell how he fixed the pump. The leather was worn out, and he managed to replace it with a piece cut out of the tongue of his shoe. He thought it might make the Hemingways feel bad if they knew the dishwater was pumped up by leather that had been worn on his foot. He saw nothing wrong with it, it was just the idea. It saved him the trouble of hunting around town for a new leather.

I went in and out of the house as I pleased, and soon began to like the place and feel at home in it. It had the front door, hall and stairs in the middle, the living room on the north side and the dining room, nook and kitchen on the south. All the furniture except the electric stove and refrigerator were antique, the dining-room table and chairs and cabinets dark brown. On the wall two stuffed partridges hung by their legs inside a round, convex glass frame and a mounted sailfish hung in the hallway opposite the stairs.

The living room, big and airy, extended the length of the building with shuttered screen doors on three sides. It was furnished with antique lounges and chairs and decorated with modernistic paintings on all the walls except the one where E. H. had his floor-to-ceiling bookshelves. The porch surrounded the house on three sides, so that any time of the day you could go out there and sit in the shade.

The only time Ernest was seen in the front room was in the winter, when it was too cold to be out on the veranda. He would sit crosslegged on a throw rug while mixing himself a drink from a bottle in the cabinet. I never saw him sit in a chair, either in his front room or any other room of his house, except at the dining-room table for the evening meal.

As a newcomer to this establishment, I could not understand all the servants. There were only four in the family, Ernest and his wife Pauline and their two young sons, Patrick and Gregory. They entertained no guests, fed no guests and slept no guests. While guests were many and frequent, they stayed elsewhere. Yet in a house where there were only four people, there were five servants, hired by the year. I made six.

Pauline worried about the WPA program turning Key West into a tourist town, on account of what it would do to the cost of keeping servants. Tourists would be competing for servants and raising wages. She liked Key West the way it was, a town everybody was leaving who could leave; those who stayed were the cheapest labor in America.

Isabelle, the cook, was proud of her job. She had been married once but was suing her husband for a divorce because he beat her up too much. Ernest engaged the divorce lawyer for $75. The husband had a reputation as a voodoo charmer. While the divorce proceedings were going on, he nearly scared the wits out of Isabelle by telling her he had a lock of her hair and was going to throw a voodoo charm on her that would take her womanhood away. E. H. had to calm her by saying, "That's nothing. I've got African lion whiskers. Nothing is as powerful as lion whiskers. If he throws any charms on you, I'll break them with the lion whiskers."

Isabelle wanted to keep her womanhood because she had a lot of it and she wanted to save it for her new lover, a sophisticated black who had been everywhere in the United States and was now the leader of the jig orchestra that played at the Bowery jitney dance, where the sailors went on Saturday and Sunday nights. He said he was cured of the wanderlust and felt like settling down and marrying Isabelle. In the afternoons, he came over and helped her scour the pots.

Louis was the tall, handsome young Negro with a soft voice who planned to become a preacher. He always wore tight blue pants and tennis shoes. He moved like a big important track star, always at a run. He came to work late in the afternoons and stayed out of sight until E. H. called, "Oh, Louis!" and then would come running easily on his long legs; "A whiskey, please, one for Mister Arnold, too," E. H. would say and Louis would disappear around the corner. In an incredibly short time he would come running back with the filled glasses on a silver tray. Louis never took a drink himself but he knew how to mix them. He used a half a dozen limes and four spoonfuls of sugar in a gin cocktail, adding more limes and sugar as long as he heard no complaints.

The washerwoman, skinny, middle-aged and black, with a whining voice, said she had never been married and had never been blessed with any children. That was all I ever found out about her.

On Monday mornings she heated a tub of water over an open fire in the back yard and rubbed the clothes by hand on a washboard. She came back on Tuesdays and sometimes Wednesdays to finish the washing and ironing. She liked me at first until she found out that I had become a member of the family and my clothes went in the wash. Since she was hired by the year, I meant extra work without extra pay and she did not like it.

Jim, the old Negro gardener, was constantly working on the lawn, cutting the grass, digging up dandelions and planting new shrubs and saying he knew where the tools were if the kids hadn't dragged them off. Jim began by calling me Mister Arnold very respectfully, just as he called E. H. Mister Ernest, but dropped the "Mister" in my case when he found out I was from the north and it wasn't necessary. Jim had trained himself to smile in front of white people even when he felt like swearing, and was always singing "Oh, all I had is gone, gone away," repeating those words over and over again in a drawling monotone, never adding any new words to it or trying to sing a different tune.

I remember Pauline spending most of her time out in the yard alongside the steel fence working with Jim. She was always telling him how to dig something up or plant something and he was saying "Yes'm." Evidently, being around Pauline so much had some effect on Jim. Twelve years after his last child was born, his wife surprised him by becoming pregnant at a time of her life when neither of them expected to be blessed in that particular way again. With another mouth to feed, he'd be blessed if he knew what he was going to do now.

Pauline was like a boy, never sitting around, always on the move. Her womanhood showed only in the twinkle of her deepset eyes and in her manicured pink fingernails and toenails. I hadn't been around much, and this was the first time I had seen a woman with manicured toenails. I could see her toenails in the sandals she wore, and they were as well kept as her fingernails.

When Pauline looked up at you and talked, she was all woman but with a tomboy's voice. She was frequently in the yard calling to somebody. "Oh, Jim." "Oh, Louis."

There was no way you could tell she was the mother of the two boys, Patrick and Gregory, five and two. She never seemed to notice them in any way. The nurse, Ada, a silent blue-eyed woman of forty, ate with the boys in the small room and taught them what not to do at the table. In the afternoons she took them for walks downtown on Duval Street to the corner drugstore for ice cream, and they would come back three abreast on the sidewalk licking their ice-cream cones. I never saw Ada smile and never heard her talk to anyone except the boys unless it was to answer a question. Ernest said she was a good nurse. All you had to do was leave her alone.

The garage under the workshop was cluttered with toys belonging to the kids. They had their toy cars, a rocking horse and a toy wagon. Other more grown-up toys were sawed-off varnished marlin spears and boxes of mounted heads. They had arrived from the taxidermist with horns mixed up and appearing on the wrong animals.

While their father was upstairs reliving hunting in Africa, they played with their toys in the shade of the workshop, making noises that did not seem to interfere with his writing. They never had any other playmates. Ernest's Key West visiting friends, the Thompsons, Dos Passos, Chambers, etc., had one thing in common: none of them had any children.

The two kids never paid the slightest attention to me. They had no interest whatever in anything that others might happen to be doing around them. They played with their toys as oblivious to spectators as animals caged in a zoo. They lived a quiet life. No laughter, no anger, no excitement. No stress of any kind. Ernest said he believed in giving the kids a calm childhood. "If they have anything," he said, "it will come out later."

Every morning, about nine o'clock, Ernest would emerge from the house and walk across the yard to begin his day's work. He would turn on the water hose to sprinkle a bare spot on the lawn and stand there watching the water squirt out. Then he'd climb the outside stairway to the door of his workshop, and at noon someone would come from the kitchen with his dinner on a tray. It was always a sandwich with a glass of tomato juice. He was working then on the beginning of what was to turn into *Green Hills of Africa*. After the day's work was finished, he would drive the Model A roadster downtown to pick up the mail.

One afternoon early in May, while E. H. and Pauline were in Miami picking up their new boat, two young men with sunburned faces came into the yard and the tallest one, who had light spots around his eyes under his glasses, shook my hand and said, "I'm Ernest's brother, Leicester. You can call me Hank. Meet my buddy, Jim Dudeck."

These two had been expected for several weeks and the newspapers had given them up as drowned. They had started out on a voyage from Mobile, Alabama, in a seventeen-foot sailboat Hank had built, intending to make Key West their first stop on a trip to South America. The boys were raised in Chicago and neither of them had ever seen salt water before or knew anything about navigation. Hank had said he could make the trip across the Gulf of Mexico in ten days, but they had been unreported for three weeks. Now they had just got in and I could see they were proud of themselves. Jim also appeared visibly relieved.

"When did you get in?" I asked.

"We just got in this afternoon," Hank said. "We were twenty-two days out of sight of land! We ran into seven bad storms! Gosh! You should have seen those waves! They were like mountains! We had to take down the sails and drag the anchor for days. Then we ran out of food and all we thought about was what we'd have to eat when we got to Key West, if we ever did. I wanted rolls and coffee, and Jim wanted a stack of hotcakes. Were we ever glad when we got here! Oh, boy! And did we stow away the grub! How long you been working for Ernest?"

"Just a few days."

"What sort of a fellow is he?"

"Why do you ask me?"

"It's funny. I've been hearing about my brother all my life and I've read all his work but I don't know him. He left home when I was six and he was only back once for a few days so I never got to know him. How did you get in with him?"

"I just dropped in to meet him and he offered me a job on his boat."

"Swell! Gosh, you're lucky! Tell me something about Ernest. I want to make a good impression on him."

"He's a damned good fellow if you don't talk too much. That's all I can say."

"I did some foolish things when I was a kid, but I want him to know I've changed. Ernest is bringing the *Pilar* in from Miami this afternoon. He'll come into the navy yard. That's where I've got the *Hawkshaw*, that's my boat. Now we're off for a swim. Why don't you come along and look her over?"

"Some other time. I've got to get this cabinet built."

"If you need any help with the cupboard, just let us know," he said as they went away.

Late that afternoon they said the *Pilar* was in, and I hurried across to the naval yard to see her. She was a beautiful thirty-eight-foot cabin cruiser, new and shiny, with a black hull, a green roof and varnished mahogany in the big cockpit and along the sides. She lay against one of the tall rotted piers built for battleships. There were many people on the dock looking down at her and E. H. was on board answering questions and showing natives through his ship.

"Well, Ernest," somebody said, "You've always wanted a boat and now, by Christ, you've got one. She's the best fishing boat in Key West."

I took my shoes off in order not to scratch the varnished deck and went aboard my new home. The cockpit was twelve feet wide and sixteen feet long, with leather-cushioned bunks on each side; the cabins below, smelling of fresh paint and alcohol from the cook stove, had a washroom, a galley with an ice box, sink, cupboards and shelves and a three-burner alcohol stove, and there were two compartments with bunks to sleep six people. E. H. said she had a stock Wheeler hull with alterations he had designed himself: a fish box built into the stern, cut down to within three feet of the water line to make it easier to gaff big fish and haul them on board; a live-bait well built under the deck; an auxiliary 40 h.p. Lycoming engine installed to run in on if the 80 h.p. marine Chrysler broke down. She was a fine boat, the most valuable property E. H. owned, and I began to think the responsibility of taking care of her might be too big for me, a young fellow who had never been on board a ship before.

"I hope everything goes all right so I can keep my job," I said, when E. H. was leaving.

"We'll see," he answered. "You sleep on her tonight. You'll find blankets and sheets in the lockers."

E. H. and Pauline drove off, the crowd of natives left, and I was alone on board a boat in a deserted navy yard. This was my new home and my new jail, in solitary confinement at times. I could see the row of empty piers, the driveway on the embankment and the palm trees in front of the buildings of the naval department and the marine hospital. Over the palm trees, I could glimpse the clock on the old courthouse tower and the roofs of other tall buildings downtown, and at the southern point of the island the old brown wall of Fort Taylor and the brush-covered mounds of dirt built over storehouses for naval supplies. Now it was May, and the nights were getting hot uptown, but it was cool enough to sleep comfortably on the water. I had a soft bunk with clean sheets and a clean blanket, and the cool salt air came through a screen that kept out the mosquitoes. In the morning, I dove off the stern and had a swim between the piers in the clear green water. I was living on a floating diving board. After a while Hank and Jim came over from the *Hawkshaw*.

"Boy! You're sure in good with Ernest!" Hank said. "We were up there for supper last night. Pauline liked the cupboard you made. She said it was swell. Boy! I wish I was in your boots. You made a swell impression on them. Ernest says I talk too much. I can't help it. I'm a conversationalist."

It seemed Hank was in trouble with his trip from Mobile. He had bragged about the seven bad storms and how he had taken down the sails and dragged the anchor for days at a time in the mountainous seas. Ernest did not like to hear this, because he had been in Key West all that time and knew it had been a month of exceptionally calm weather. Hank had taken down his sail and dragged anchor in fear of his life every time he had a sailing breeze and raised the sails only in calms, and that was why it had taken him twenty-two days on a trip that he could have made in a week. Hank was fond of argument and stuck to his storms; that was why he failed to made a good impression and now he wished he was me.

In retrospect, Ernest's younger brother expected a hero's welcome and probably deserved it. Certainly that voyage, with another amateur youth from Chicago, neither of them with previous sea experience, sailing out of sight of land across five hundred miles of water, heading for a distant island, which, if they had missed, would have stranded them in the ocean, that voyage for guts and seamanship by his kid brother beat everything Ernest would ever do on board the *Pilar,* which at all times had a veteran seaman familiar with the coast and the waters on board.

Hank and the *Hawkshaw* had been honored upon his arrival by being the first private yacht admitted to the Key West Naval Basin, previously restricted to the navy and coastguard vessels. That honor had been granted by Lieutenant Jackson, commandant of the submarine base. Hank had been granted this honor because he was the brother of Ernest Hemingway, not for his sailing prowess. His mother in Chicago had some money for him after his graduation from high school, from a trust fund Ernest had given her from the movie rights for *A Farewell to Arms.* Hank preferred not to go to college. Instead, he elected to use the money to go to Mobile, Alabama, where he spent six months building the *Hawkshaw.*

Around nine o'clock, Hemingway's Model A roadster, with the sun shining through the block of ice on the rear bumper, came running smoothly over the black road of the dock, slowing down and turning in at the pier, then rattling over the loose planks and stopping above us. The old man with Hemingway was Captain Bra Saunders, a fishing guide who owned his own party boat. He was a true Conch with a lean, reddish face, pale, watery eyes and a long nose coming straight down from a high forehead. They got out, leaving the doors open, and E. H., big and healthy and in a good humor, looked down at his boat.

"Good morning, gentlemen," he said.

"Hi, Stein!" Hank shouted.

"We're going fishing."

"Oh, boy!"

They handed down the ice, wicker fishing chairs from the house, a cardboard box full of beer bottles, a bottle of gin and one of whiskey, a lunch basket, mullet bait wrapped in newspaper and fishing rods and tackle. Captain Bra took off his shoes and came down barefoot. E. H. drove off and returned later with Pauline and Archibald MacLeish, the poet, a handsome athlete wearing a striped sweater. In another roadster, Karl Thompson, Hemingway's hunting companion in Africa, a big, awkward fellow with a wrinkled face, came with his wife, Lorine, a schoolteacher.*

The men helped the women down off the pier and came on board. E. H. stepped on the buttons that started both motors and Captain Bra, having cast off the ropes, turned the *Pilar* around between the piers, shoving ahead and backing up several times until he was clear, and headed her out of the navy yard through the opening in the wall of the breakwater, turning to the left on a southward course toward the Gulf Stream.

The sea was green and flat over the reef and the boat ran along smoothly. E. H. was happy at the wheel. It was a beautiful, clear day, and he was going out for the sport he loved in the best fishing grounds in the world at the wheel of his own boat, which was built just as he had wanted her built, with bunks enough to sleep eight people if they cared to stay out overnight on the keys, and small enough to turn on her rudder and follow a marlin. A boat like this was something he had always wanted and now he had her, she would last a lifetime if he took care of her, which he would, and he saw many happy days of fishing and big fish ahead.

"It's a bloody marvelous day, isn't it?" he said to Pauline.

"It's lovely," she said.

"How do you feel, Mummy?"

"Fine. I couldn't feel any better."

"Are you quite comfortable?"

"This is splendid."

"You won't get seasick today, Mummy. It'll be even better when we get out past the tide rip."

"Oh, I think this is grand."

---

* *Ed. note:* Karl was the fictionalized name of Charles Thompson in *Green Hills*, and this became his nickname.

"She's a good sea boat, isn't she, Mummy? See how she takes the swells?"

"It's marvelous."

Captain Bra bent down on one knee and began scaling and slicing mullet for bait. Each mullet made two streamlined strips, which he laid out flat on ice, scaly side down. Wire leaders were fastened to the lines. Two wooden teasers, one green, the other white, were tossed over the stern and towed on twenty-foot lines. Ernest said the white teaser, more easily seen, would raise the fish at a greater distance, while up close they preferred the green one.

The cockpit was crowded, with Lorine lying on one of the bunks anticipating seasickness, Captain Bra kneeling on the floor slicing mullet, Hank and Jim sitting on the fishbox astern, Archie in one of the fishing chairs and Karl and I standing.

"Let's put out a feather, Cap," E. H. told Bra. "You put one out, Karl."

"No, I don't want to fish just yet," Karl said. "Somebody else fish."

"Go ahead, Karl."

"I'll wait till somebody else catches one."

"You catch one for us, Mr. Thompson," Pauline said.

"No, true, I'd rather see somebody else catch a fish," protested Karl. "Mr. MacLeish, you fish."

"Here's one with a feather on, if anybody likes to fish," Captain Bra said, tossing the feather overboard and slacking line until it trailed a long way astern near the surface.

"Archie, you put it out then," E. H. said. "Cap, put on a spoon for Karl."

Bra soon had the spoon ready and offered Karl the other rod.

"No, let Leicester fish. You take it, Leicester," Karl said.

"Hank hasn't ever fished with a reel," E. H. said. "Let him watch somebody else first."

"You fish, Ernest."

"No, I'll put you over one."

"Lorine?"

"Not yet," Lorine answered.

"Put her out, Karl," E. H. said, and Karl had to fish. Karl cared nothing for fishing. He was raised in Key West, and he had had enough of it. The Thompson family enterprises included a hardware store and tackle shop, an icehouse, a ship's chandlery, a cigarbox factory, a turtle cannery, a pineapple factory and a fishery, including the fishing boats. He knew more about fishing around the Keys than many of the local Conches would know in a lifetime. He preferred riding in airplanes and eating beef. "Airplanes have always spooked me," Ernest told me later. "I wouldn't do what Karl is doing for ten thousand dollars."

Both motors were humming, swiftly pushing Key West astern until only the radio towers and the La Concha Hotel were distinctly visible. E. H. unfolded a Key West chart on the panel in front of the wheel. He showed me the buoys and other landmarks on the chart, and then pointed to them on the water. On our first run out he was teaching me.

"There's Sand Key lighthouse straight ahead, see it?"

"No."

"Look where I'm pointing."

"Oh, yes. Now I see it."

"That's seven miles from Key West. We run into the Gulf Stream on the other side. See the small stake to the left? That's the Eastern Dry Rocks. You can see the water breaking white near the stake. That's how you can tell a sandbar. You can see it better when there's a breeze."

"What makes the different colors on the water?"

"The bottom. The dark-purple patches are where there's seaweed, it's green where there's coral and you'll see the brownish color near the Dry Rocks where there's sand. Being out on the water is good training for your eyes."

"I'd think you'd get lost out here."

"You get used to the landmarks and you always know where you're at."

"What if you broke down and it got dark?"

"You'd have the lights."

"But if it got foggy so you couldn't see?"

"It never gets foggy here, but if it rains you've got your binnacle to run in by."

"Would there be danger then of running into one of those buoys?"

"There might if you couldn't see the lights or didn't know the chart."

Past the Sand Key lighthouse, E. H. told me when we were going over the sixty-fathom bar and, looking down, I could see the coral bottom drop off and the water change from green to a clear blue.

"Now we're in deeper water," he said. "Look ahead and you can see the Gulf Stream. See that purple line where the birds are?"

"No. I don't even see the birds."

"You've got to get your eyes used to the water before you can see anything. Look straight ahead."

"Now I see the birds."

"That's the edge of the stream, that darker water. See that glossy path? That's made by the current flowing against the tide from the reef. It's filled with patches of seaweed. Now you can see the flying fish, hundreds of them! I'll bet we hook into one today, what do you say, Cap?"

"Yeah, I think so, Ernest," Bra said.

"That's what you look for, flying fish and birds. Whenever you see flying fish you know there's bigger fish chasing them up, and the terns and gulls catch them in the air. See the man-of-war hawk, flying up there above the other birds? He isn't any good on the water and he can't catch his own fish. He takes them away from the other birds in the air."

"It seems like a massacre is going on here all the time."

"It's the same on land, except that it isn't so obvious. Hi! A sailfish! Look at him jump!" Ernest shouted, pointing ahead. We watched where he pointed. The sailfish came up again eight or nine times, stiff as a silvery sword. He danced on his tail and shook his bill.

"Toss out a bait! Get out the teasers!" E. H. told Bra. "Let's see if he'll strike."

We made a few circles, trolling the baits over the place where the fish made his last jump, but he did not show up again. E. H. steered the *Pilar* across the slick and followed it far enough on the stream side to avoid the seaweed, with the bow headed into the hot sun and his guests fishing in the cool shade of the cockpit roof.

"What made the sailfish jump like that?" I asked.

"He's got suckerfish in his gills. He was trying to shake them off," E. H. answered.

"We've seen one already. Is that a good sign?"

"No. Not enough wind. On calm days the surface water is warm and the big fish stay deep down except when they come up to shake off the suckerfish, so when you don't see them jumping you have a much better chance of catching a sailfish. How do you feel, Mummy?"

"Wonderful," she said.

"Isn't it a bloody marvelous day out here on the stream?"

"It's lovely."

"Look how blue the water is."

"It's beautiful."

"Plenty cool out here, isn't it?"

"Everything's just perfect."

Archie's rod whipped and his line suddenly ran vibrating off his clicking reel into the blue water.

"Pull him in. It's a bonito," E. H. said, cutting down the motor. "You can tell the way he fights. Work him in fast."

A barracuda clipped the bonito's tail off and came back after another chunk, leaving only the head on the hook when Archie brought it in.

"Shit, too slow," E. H. said. "You've got to work them in fast."

"Now it's your turn, Ernest."

"No. Go ahead and catch a whole one."

In fifteen minutes Archie caught two cero mackerel and Karl caught a bonito and a twenty-pound barracuda. What impressed me most was Hemingway's incredible eyesight. He sometimes saw the fish take the bait and told us what it was before the man at the rod knew he had a strike, or if he happened to be looking ahead when the fish struck and sounded, he could tell by the way it pulled what sort of a fish and how big it was. Captain Bra reached the wire leader with his canvas glove and pulled the flopping mackerel on board carelessly, but he was afraid of Karl's barracuda. It was silvery with black spots, a pointed head and a mouth full of teeth shaped like a police dog's. One snap of those jaws could chop off a man's wrist. Bra held the leader as far away from him as his arm would reach and clubbed the fish as it swung back and forth, careful not to touch it until it stopped jerking and hung straight, and not feeling safe until the hook was out and the barracuda dropped into the fish box.

"What's the matter, Cap?" E. H. asked. "You afraid of them?"

"No, I'm not afraid," Bra said. "Just careful. That's all. I've seen too much. I saw a dead barracuda rip a man's leg open."

"How did that happen?"

"Dropped him when its mouth was open and one of its teeth caught in his pants. Them teeth is sharp. Ripped him right down the leg. Doctor had to sew him up with stitches. Want me to take the wheel, Ernest?"

"No, I'd just as soon look for them." E. H. did not care to fish for what could be caught on this side of the Gulf Stream. He got no kick out of these little fish.

At noon we drank beer off the ice, opened the lunch basket and ate fried spring chickens, deviled eggs and mayonnaise sandwiches wrapped in wax paper. The food tasted very good out on the open water.

In the afternoon we trolled slowly into the sun. E. H. stayed at the wheel watching for birds and flying fish, Captain Bra unhooked the fish caught and put on fresh bait for Karl, Archie, Pauline and Lorine, who sometimes changed off at the rods. E. H. said Hank, Jim and I ought to wait and see how it was done before we tried it.

The high point came late in the afternoon when Karl and Archie both had strikes, and suddenly hundreds of yellowish-green dolphins appeared on the surface close to the boat. It was the largest school of dolphin Captain Bra had ever seen. E. H. shut down the motor and ran astern shouting "Grab the teasers, quick!" He threw pieces of bait overboard to keep the dolphins interested while Karl and Archie were reeling and pumping in their fish and Bra was hauling in the teasers. E. H. grabbed another rod, put a piece of bait on the hook and handed it to me. I threw the bait over and saw a dolphin snatch it off the hook before I had time to strike.

"Too slow," E. H. laughed, putting on another bait. "Try again."

I threw over again and the same thing happened. I lost seven or eight fish before I finally caught two. The dolphins struck the baits as fast as we could throw them over, and we kept pulling them in, Bra and E. H. taking them off and rebaiting the hooks. E. H. threw out scraps of mullet to keep them interested; when there was no mullet left, he threw out pieces of newspaper wiped in fish slime and they struck at the floating papers.

The dolphins disappeared as suddenly as they had come, and when the excitement was over we found that we had taken eighteen in five minutes, the heaviest weighing about thirty pounds; we could hear their tails drumming the sides of the fish box. They would go up to the house grounds for fertilizer for Pauline's plants.

"How's that for a haul, Cap?" Ernest asked.

"Not bad, Ernest. Don't you think we better have a drink on that, hey?"

"Mix them up, Cap."

Bra mixed the whiskies and, as the sun was getting low, we reeled in and started back over the reef toward Key West, both motors hooked up and the bow pointed toward the radio towers of the naval yard. That was the first fishing day for Ernest Hemingway on the *Pilar*.

2

Lessons

DURING THE FIRST two weeks, there was such an epidemic of guests that Ernest did not get a chance to fish much. The guests knew very little about sailfishing and he had to tell them what to do and correct their mistakes. With guests at the rods, the fish, once hooked, were in command, and Ernest had to chase them with the boat. The *Pilar* always put up a good fight, but E. H. said it was a crime to make the boat fight the fish.

On windy days when the sea got rough I became seasick and lost all interest in fishing. Ernest said it would be smoother riding in the forward cockpit and the salt spray would do me good. I felt the boat sink slowly and then suddenly lunge ahead with the waves. It seemed alive, as if it propelled itself with the strokes of a powerful swimmer.

The wind came from the southeast, the ebbing tide from the north, and the Gulf current from the west. These contending forces gave me a dizzy ride. When I thought nobody was watching I leaned over the rail, with all the sensations of a terrific hangover. I sat forward, with no interest in what was going on, the whole afternoon, wondering why I had thought there was salt in my blood.

Hank, who was palefaced and just as sick as I was, used to go down into the cabin and sit under the table, with his head between his knees, trying to sleep. Hank always felt nauseated because he was too proud to heave. His reputation as a sailor of the seven bad storms was at stake.

Archie felt it too, but he held it down and sat trolling the strip bait, looking astern through his dark glasses, never turning his head and never saying a word to anybody all afternoon. We had the most action in the roughest weather, when the boat was pitching so much we could hardly stand on our feet without holding on to something and the bad sailors were all seasick.

Fishing continued every day because Archie was down on vacation as a special guest for this event, and E. H. was determined to make him catch a sailfish. "Archie can write poetry," Ernest told me, "but poetry is easy. If a poet hits it lucky, he can write two lines and live forever. What is hard is prose."

We fished with the drags off, holding the loose spools with our thumbs, and E. H. told us to slack to anything because it was difficult for a beginner to tell the tap of a sailfish bill from the slap of a wave or the jerk of seaweed caught on the hook. He said the reason for slacking was to let the bait stop like a fish that had been stunned or killed so the sailfish might come back after it, and the time to strike was when the sailfish was running off with the bait well in his mouth. A strike too soon would jerk the bait out of his jaws. If too late, he might have felt the hook and started jumping clear of the water on a slack line and throw the bait out of his mouth before there was any chance to strike. He told us how to keep a fingertip on the spool while slacking line to avoid a backlash, and stop it completely before putting on the drag. E. H. explained these things until we had a good understanding of what to do when we were calm and could think about it, but it was different when we were seasick and excited and heard E. H. at the wheel shouting, "Hi! A sailfish! He's after you, Archie! Now he's after you, Jim! Get ready to slack to him. Don't strike until I tell you. There! He hit it! Slack to him! *Slack to him!!!* Shit! Why the hell didn't you slack to him? He's spooked now and he never will come back." The E. H.–MacLeish friendship was never the same after that.

We were all alike when we saw a sailfish after our baits, getting excited and striking when E. H. told us to slack or slacking too late or with too much drag on or else not touching the spool at all and having the line tangled in a backlash and snapped off. Or we did not work the fish in fast enough. Anything can happen when the fish is still in the water, and E. H. told us we should always try to kill them as fast as possible without being rough. It was all in knowing what tension we could use and when to apply it. Archie had eight sailfish strikes but did not get his hook into the mouth of any of them because he could not learn the trick of slacking. After ten days he left Key West without a sailfish.

Hank lost ten that he failed to hook and two by not working them into the boat fast enough and not keeping the line taut, giving them a chance to throw the hook when they jumped with their mouths open. Once he struck back too far, slamming an eighty-dollar rod against the cockpit roof and breaking it off in the middle when he had a fish on; the fish broke the line and got away. E. H. never said a word about the rod. Hank said the rod was no good.

Jim hooked a beautiful sailfish that flung itself clear of the water, a dozen times, stood upright dancing on its tail and, shaking its head, went down for a fast run, whipping line off the spool.

"Stop him. For chrissake, stop him!" E. H. shouted from the wheel. The fish had nearly all the line out before Jim could turn him. "Now bring him in. If you can hold him you can get line on him. Remember, it's the fish that's got the hook in his mouth. You don't have to kill him. Convince him. Don't try to reel him in. You can't. Pump him. That's what the rod is for. Then reel in as you lower it. Don't lower the rod any faster than you can reel in, or you'll give him slack."

E. H. had the boat running backward toward the fish. Jim reeled in a few feet and lost a few yards and the tug of war kept on for twenty minutes until E. H. shouted, "Blood! A shark's got him. Oh, shit!" The shark struck three times and the third time Jim had a 200-pound shark on instead of a sailfish. The shark did not fight hard and Jim led it to the stern, where E. H. gaffed it and shot it in the head. When it was hauled on board, E. H. cut it open and found the sailfish in three chunks inside the shark's belly and nine unborn little sharks about two feet long, perfectly formed and slimy, that wriggled and tried to swim when they fell on the dry deck. E. H. stuck the knife through their heads and threw them over with their dead mother and we watched them swim off to die.

E. H. said he would like to see a sample of my work, so I gave him one of the newspaper articles I had written while hoboing in the West, the one about being stranded all night on a ledge of a cliff, which an editor had praised as the best of the lot.

"I read your piece," E. H. told me the next day when we went fishing. "It's nothing to worry about. I wrote some stuff as bad as that when I was your age. Every writer does. They all have to learn to write. If a writer sells his first story, that's the most unfortunate thing that can happen to him, because if he can sell shit he might keep on writing shit, and even if he does get better the readers always remember him by their first impression."

When E. H. was in the mood to talk about writing was the happiest time I had, and now he was at the wheel steering over the reef toward Sand Key lighthouse and I stood beside him in the open doorway to the cabins.

"The first stuff you write doesn't mean a damned thing. I had one of the best newspaper jobs in Europe, writing under two different names with two salaries and two expense accounts, and when I had saved enough money to quit the newspapers and take a chance on fiction, I wrote for two years and didn't sell a damned thing. I kept sending them off and when they sent them back they wouldn't even call them stories. They called them sketches. Then when I left Paris I had all my stuff in a suitcase. My wife lost the suitcase somewhere on the way and I never did get it back. At first I couldn't realize what had happened. I had lost two year's work, and once I write a thing and get it the way I want it I forget about it and can't remember it afterward. I didn't realize it then, but that was the most fortunate thing that could have happened to me, because now the critics don't know what I wrote first and they can't trace my development. It's none of their business that you have to learn to write. Let them think you were born that way."

"Didn't you save any of it?"

"Only three stories that were in the mail. 'My Old Man,' 'The Undefeated' and 'Fifty Grand.' Every damned one came back. They didn't want them. Afterward I sold 'Fifty Grand' to the *Atlantic Monthly* and the editors who had sent my stuff back began to write letters asking me to send *them* something. If they were magazines that couldn't pay I never answered, and I held up the others for a dollar a word and sent them the same 'sketches' they had sent back when they could have had them for nothing.

"If they send your stuff back, that doesn't mean a thing. It's to be expected. If you don't write like everybody else does, the readers in the magazine offices don't know you're good until somebody else makes the discovery and then they all see it at once. If you write poor stuff, you can keep on sending it off and it will always come back, but if you write good stuff and keep it in the mails, someday somebody will buy it. The first crap you write doesn't mean a thing. Everybody has to learn. You don't have a thing to worry about. I never had anybody to teach me about writing, and it took me years to find out for myself what I'll be telling you now."

"I had a letter from George Peterson," I said. "He's the Sunday editor of the Minneapolis *Tribune* and he wanted me to write an interview with you for his book page."

"I didn't know that was what you wanted," E. H. said, thoughtfully.

"No, I didn't have that in mind. He wrote after I'd seen you."

"I'd let you write an interview if it would help you out any on your career, but the reason I don't ever give interviews is the interviewers forget what I say and make up something pretty of their own. How much does the *Tribune* pay?"

"I only got fifteen bucks for nine long articles."

"Then it wouldn't be worth much to you in money."

"No, I told him I couldn't write it."

"You'll get something better later on."

"Would you care if I tried to write something about fishing with you?"

"Hell, no. You can make me out any kind of a son of a bitch you want when we get back from Cuba. That's your privilege."

I ran a splinter into my knee climbing the pier one morning, and two days later it began to swell with an infection. When I told E. H., he immediately took me to Dr. Warren and had the bill charged to his account. The doctor lanced the sore and said the leg should not be used until it got well. It was painful only when I walked, but E. H. felt very sorry for me. He drove me home, had me made comfortable on one of his padded chairs on the veranda with my foot raised on a high stool, and told me not to move—his servants would bring me anything I wanted. He brought me some newspapers and magazines to read and in the afternoon when he had gone fishing, after I had awoke from a short nap, Pauline came to see how I was getting along and the long-legged Negro, Louis, brought me a gin cocktail with lime and bitters.

"What makes you think you want to be a writer?" Pauline asked suddenly.

"I don't know," I said. "I can't tell you."

"If I had to have a writer in the family, I'd want him to be a good one."

"I'd like to be a good one."

"Then you can't just write about moonlight."

"I've never tried to write about moonlight."

"So many of them do. What would you do if you couldn't sell anything?"

"I suppose I'd live cheap and keep trying."

"What would you do for money?"

"I don't need much."

"The best things in life aren't free. You'll find that out. I want what I want when I want it."

"I suppose it depends on what you want. It won't be hard for me to get what I'm used to."

"Don't mind me. I'm just in a mood to argue. But I'm tired of the starving artist type that wastes away in attics, and I don't like the proud poor. You can't do anything for them. I had some new dresses I couldn't use, and I tried to give them to some needy girls, but do you suppose they'd take them? They were too proud, and the only person I could give the dresses to was one who had money and could easily afford to buy anything she needed."

"I'm not very proud. I'll take all the dresses you got."

"How does your knee feel?"

"It feels fine now when it's rested. I'm glad it got hurt."

"Why?"

"I needed a rest from being seasick."

"You'll get over that."

"It must be rough out in the stream now, the way the wind is blowing through the palm trees. I would have been seasick today too."

"You weren't sick the first days."

"Then it wasn't so rough."

"Can I have Louis get you another gin?"

"No, thanks."

"Are you sure you don't want another?"

"Pretty sure."

"Positive?"

"I might if you insist."

She called Louis and had him bring me another.

"Is there anything else you'd like to read?" she asked.

"Yes, I'd like something by Ernest Hemingway."

"What have you read?"

"*A Farewell to Arms* and 'One Trip Across.' "

"I'll see what I can find."

She found two books, *In Our Time* and *The Torrents of Spring*, and then I was alone again in the shade of the porch, listening to the wind shake the long blades of the palm trees and reading the books I had been wanting to read by Ernest Hemingway in the home of Ernest Hemingway. It seemed odd.

3

The Priest and the Sailfish

A MIDDLE-AGED PRIEST who was an ardent fisherman but badly crippled with arthritis came to Key West on duty, but he had planned to work in a trip with E. H., too.

He had his own slender rod and reel and he declined the mullet bait, preferring his sparkling array of gadgets. He said he didn't want a sailfish. They were too big for him. E. H. told me he was a very fine bait caster and he liked to use bait-casting tackle out in the Gulf.

He trolled a long while before he got a strike. The barracuda made a spectacular bend in his slender rod. He gave Ernest his Kodak, thoughtfully kept near at hand, to take a picture of the bending rod. He got the picture, but the barracuda went off with his silverware. He lost a lot of silverware.

The priest went away for a few days and came back for another afternoon's fishing. That day I did not go along, being laid up with my knee. In the evening, I was driven down to meet the boat. She came in late, a sailfish flag waving at the mast.

Pauline asked, "Who caught the fish?"

There was a suspicious silence. Ernest pointed his thumb at the priest. The sailfish was lying on the deck. It looked enormous, and in fact, measured with a steel tape, was nine feet and three quarters of an inch long, heavy and rounded all the way to its tail.

I stayed on the boat while the group took the fish off to be weighed. Jim Dudeck came back with the news. The sailfish weighed 119½ pounds. It was the largest ever taken on the Atlantic coast, the previous record of twelve years ago being ninety-eight pounds. Who caught the fish? The priest? It seemed impossible to me. Ernest said he was a swell fisherman, but I had seen enough sailfish caught by now to know what one that size meant.

Dudeck cleared up the mystery.

Father McGrath was trolling with Ernest's rod and a reel that was in rather bad shape. He had already lost one sailfish to a shark after a good fight, and his back was tired. The fish he lost jumped fifteen times and he fought him half an hour. It was sundown, and they were coming in from the stream. Near the Western Dry Rocks the priest had a strike, and they saw the giant sailfish leap like a marlin and come down with a splash in the wake of the boat. Seeing the sailfish, the priest yelled to Ernest, "You take it!"

"No," Ernest replied. "I don't want it. He's your fish."

The sail was in command, taking out line. The reel was about run out, with the boat after him. The priest hung on for two minutes, putting up a good fight, but finally he said, "My back's too bad. Take him, Ernest. Please!"

As it was apparent that he was really suffering from his back, E. H. took the rod. The sail had nearly all the line out. There was only 140 yards of old line, spliced in three places. The reel was an old-style Templar, and E. H., taking the drag lever off and using his thumb for a brake so he could tell exactly what tension he was applying, worked the fish to the stern in fifteen minutes.

The guide, a substitute for Captain Bra that day, missed with the gaff, raking the fish in the side. The sail went under the boat and Ernest quickly leaned over the stern and passed the rod, reel and all, into the water, the drag free to let the fish go down and clear the propeller. A second later and the line would have been cut off on the propeller. Four times he brought the fish up close and, the guide missing with the gaff, it dove under the boat. Each time Ernest cleared the propeller, keel and rudder by the same maneuver. At the fifth approach of the fish the guide gaffed him, and so ended the battle that had waged forty-two minutes.

The men at the scales wanted to know who would claim the record sailfish. Ernest told the priest to take all the honor. The priest refused, but he was in a quandary. More than anything else, he would have liked the distinction of having hooked a record fish. But if he accepted the credit it would be in the papers, and his orders had been that fishing was okay but fishing publicity was not. He would not accept credit for hooking the fish. E. H. wouldn't claim it either, which resulted in the quandary of the unclaimed record sailfish of the Atlantic.

After hearing Dudeck describe this fight, I could believe there was much truth in the stories about large fish that got away in the Gulf. Like the record fish that crossed underneath the boat, they are liable to present difficult situations the amateur cannot cope with, and he brings back only a story, one which people often scoff at.

Contrary to popular opinion, E. H. believed there were as many sailfish in the stream in summer as in winter. They were much fatter and in better condition, since they had not spawned and they put up a greater fight. In the month of June, the *Pilar*, despite the number of amateurs at the rods, brought in twelve sailfish in eleven and a half days of fishing.

4

How to Write the Stuff

E. H. HAD STARTED to write a short story about Africa to give Scribner's a new, unpublished tale they wanted for an omnibus edition of his works, but the story grew longer than he expected and it was now seventy-five pages and looked as if it might turn into a book. E. H. wrote every forenoon, and in the afternoons we went fishing in the stream in good weather. When it was too rough, we stayed in the harbor tied between the piers, and E. H. came down to start the motors and charge the batteries. One windy afternoon he came on board and found a book that had been in the library at his house called *The Writing Racket* by Jack Woodford.

"Who's been reading this crap?" he asked.

"I brought it down yesterday," Hank said. "I thought you wouldn't mind."

"If you want to be a writer, you don't want to read that stuff," E. H. said. "It's just a lot of shit. I never bought the book. The bastard sent it to me. He tells about slanting your stories for the different magazines, doesn't he?"

"Yes."

"That's just a lot of shit. I never slanted a story in my life. You slant your journalism because you make your living that way, but if you want to be any good at it, never slant a fiction story for any magazine. I never think of publication until I've finished a story. Write a story exactly the way you think it ought to be written, not as the editor would want it.

"I remember Scott Fitzgerald used to tell me how he slanted stories for the *Saturday Evening Post* and how much they paid him. All Scott ever got out of writing was a few bottles of whiskey and a few hotel rooms. It would burn him up if he knew what they're paying me. I had a letter from young George Lorimer a while ago, offering me five thousand for anything I'd care to write. It needn't be long. Anything over a thousand words."

"What did you tell him?" I asked.

"I never answered his letter."

"Why not?"

"You can always sell out. I was broke when I got the offer, but I wasn't that hard up. I was broke once before, when Hearst sent me a check for twenty-five thousand as an offer for *A Farewell to Arms,* and I sent the check back and let Scribner's have the story. That check was damned tempting and I needed the money, but I'm glad now that I sent it back. The way it turned out, I got more money out of the book than if I'd let Hearst have it. You can always popularize your stuff, but if you do, you can't keep your price up. Besides being a damned poor policy for a writer, it's bad business.

"I was broke when I came back from Africa this spring and Paramount sent me an offer of ten thousand a week to come out there for five weeks while they were making a war picture. I wouldn't have anything to do with the picture. They'd just use my name."

"What did you tell them?"

"I never answered them."

"Why not?"

"That impresses them. If I ever write another novel, when they want the movie rights they'll think in terms of big money.

"Don't ever slant your fiction. The only reason editors publish slanted stories is because that's the kind the writers keep on sending them; when they put their stories in a book, the book doesn't sell. I get more money for my stuff than they do, and when I publish a collection of short stories the book sells because people want to read them. Good stuff always pays. It might not at first, but it always does in the end.

"The readers know a good story but the editors don't. If you submit a story that is different, the editors don't see it. If you've got a good story, don't even look at it when it comes back. Just keep sending it off. If it's good, some editor will notice it, and after one sees it, the others do. But if it's a bad story, you can keep sending it around forever and nobody will buy it.

"If you ever sell a story, it might just be an accident and it might take years before you ever sell another one. For that reason, don't quit what you are doing to make a living. Don't ever worry about not having friends. If you make money, you'll have all the friends you want. And if you ever make any real money, whatever you do, don't get carried away. That's their way of destroying you."

"I read a little in that book, too," I confessed. "Woodford said when you write a novel you ought to make an outline of the plot and divide it into chapters before you start writing."

Hemingway sat down on the bunk, bringing his legs under him and sitting on his heels, and waved his arm as if throwing something away from his face.

"That's horseshit! If you use an outline, the reader can tell it. The story is forced and unnatural. Sometimes you think you know how a story is going to end, but when you get to writing it, it turns out entirely different. Anybody knows when he gets to the end of a chapter. I never divide a book into chapters until I'm through writing it. A lot of rackets have started in the Depression, and one of the worst is the writing racket, phony writers who advertise they can teach people to write and make a lot of money. If they know how to do it, why the hell don't they go ahead and do it themselves?"

"Woodford said when a man's writing a novel he absolutely shouldn't have any sexual intercourse. Is that true?"

"Not always. Sometimes it clears the head."

"When you read a story, can you tell if the writer has had inter-course?"

"Instantly!"

"How about liquor?"

"A little is all right if you know how to drink, because it puts your mind on a different plane and it changes your ideas. But you always want to drink after you're through, not before or while you're writing."

"Another thing Woodford said in his book was that a writer ought to start with the newspaper syndicates and the pulps."

"That's absolutely wrong! Don't believe that crap. If you want to be a writer, make your money writing journalism or in any other way, but for chrissake don't depend on fiction for your living. If you start in writing phony stuff for the pulps, chances are you'll never learn how to write anything else. I've known a lot of pulp writers who thought they'd keep on until they'd saved enough money to live on and then write good stuff, but it never works. They find out they've never learned how to write. All they've been writing is shit and they've got so they can't write anything different. Their reputations as pulp writers don't amount to a damn and some day they either find they've written themselves out and they can't sell their stuff, or else they simply get disgusted and quit.

"The way to learn how to write is to write a lot of journalism first because that limbers you up and gives you a command of the language. Then practice with daily exercises. Every day describe something you've seen so that the reader can see it and it becomes alive on paper. That's the way Flaubert taught Maupassant to write. Describe anything—the car on the dock, a squall on the stream or a heavy sea. Then try to get the emotion. If you fellows want to write daily exercises, I'll be glad to look them over and tell you what's wrong with them."

"Gosh! That would be swell!" said Hank, who wanted to be a journalist.

"They ought to have me teach some of those college classes. I could teach them something. Most professors of English composition can tell the students what's wrong with their pieces but they don't know how to made them good, because, if they knew that, they'd be writers themselves and they wouldn't have to teach."

"What do you think of the life of a professor?"

"All right for a person who is vain and likes to have the adulation of his students. Well, now, do you fellows think you can remember everything Professor Hemingway has told you? Are you prepared for a written examination on the lecture?"

"I hope the wind drops off so we can fish tomorrow. This breeze ought to bring them up."

5

Visiting Fishermen

THE NEXT MORNING E. H. came on board with Pauline. He was dressed up in white trousers instead of khakis and Captain Bra was not along, so I knew we would not be going fishing. He started the motors and told me to cast off the ropes and steered the *Pilar* out of the navy yard toward the Havana Ferry depot.

"Have you ever heard of John Charles Thomas?" he asked me.

"No. Who is he?"

"A singer. Pauline's heard of him but I haven't. We're going over to see him."

We headed for a big white yacht lying at anchor in the harbor near the depot. Mr. Thomas had a floating palace. A slim woman in black bloomers stood at the rail waving her arm stiffly as we came up. We ran the *Pilar* alongside and men in blue uniforms caught our ropes, tied the boats together with bumpers between them and lowered a gangplank for E. H. and Pauline to go on board. E. H. had a manuscript envelope filled with pictures he had taken in Africa. E. H. and Pauline climbed on board, and Hank and I stayed on the *Pilar* as they shook hands with the woman and disappeared through one of the doors. While the Hemingways were socializing with the Thomases, the crew for the yacht came on board the *Pilar* to look her over. The crew consisted of a big Negro and a white man, who opened the doors of the engine pit and argued about the purpose of having the small auxiliary Lycoming motor as well as the big one, agreeing it was foolish. The Negro went through the cabins and examined everything critically, he being from a bigger yacht. They went off when E. H. and Pauline came down the gangplank followed by the slim woman wearing dark glasses and the black bloomers, a pretty blond girl and a short, stout man with a round face and a close haircut, who walked with his chest out and his head back: John Charles Thomas. The slim woman was his wife and the other the daughter of his Swiss singing teacher, an old man with a pointed gray beard who had taught Thomas before he became famous, and who was now living on the yacht with his daughter, still as a voice coach to Thomas. Hemingway was unusually alert, observing everything through his thick glasses and talking loud and cheerfully with Thomas while showing him the cabins, engines, fish box, live-bait well and gasoline tanks.

"Isn't she roomy?" E. H. said.

Thomas cleared his throat.

"Very beamy. Very comfortable. She has much more room than you'd think."

"She'll sleep eight people if we ever want to stay out."

"How is she on the water?"

"She's a good seaboat. We'll take her out for a ride."

E. H. started both motors and hooked up full speed ahead over the reef.

"Plenty fast, isn't she?"

Thomas cleared his throat again. "Very good."

"She'll do sixteen knots on both motors. Now that I've cut off the little one, you don't get the vibration. The big one is rubber mounted. This is trolling speed. Doesn't she run quiet?"

"Yes, indeed."

"Now, see how you can cut her down. She stops in her length and idles in gear with the propeller moving. That way, when you hook into a big fish, you can stop and have her ready to start ahead instantly. All you've got to do is to push the gas lever."

"That's quite a system."

"This is the sort of boat you ought to get for fishing. You could take her in tow just as easily as your open boat and it wouldn't cost much more to run."

"I might at that. You've got a swell boat here."

"How about a drink? Do you think it's time for a drink?"

"It's always time for a drink," Thomas said.

"All right, Arnold. Let's have a drink."

This was my first attempt at drink mixing. I went below and mixed a whiskey for E. H., one for myself and a gin cocktail with lime and sugar and chipped ice and soda water for Thomas, who thanked me as he took the glass and raised it to his thin lips. He took a sip and exclaimed, "What is this? Lemonade?"

"Gin," I said.

"Can you taste any gin in this," he asked, giving me a drink from his glass.

"No, I don't taste it."

"That's what I thought."

"Maybe I forgot to put some in."

"Some bartender!" E. H. said, laughing. "He mixes a gin drink without any gin in it."

"Would it be all right if I put some gin in it?"

"I'd like it much better that way," Thomas said. "Much better."

I took his glass below, poured two fingers of gin in it and brought it back up.

"Ah, yes, this is much better," Thomas said. "It's really surprising what a difference a little gin will make."

We took a trip over the reef to the mud banks, where the hull of a wrecked ship was lying upside down with its keel above the shallow water. Late in the afternoon we circled the island and came in at the naval yard and tied to the pier.

"How about a swim?" E. H. suggested.

"I love the water," Thomas said. "But we've heard so much about sharks and barracuda down here."

"Nobody's ever been struck and we go in every day. The naval yard is really a good place to swim. The water's clear and you hardly ever see any seaweed floating in here as it is now. It blew in last night."

"I'd like to go in if it's safe."

"It's absolutely safe."

We went below to put on our trunks, came up and dove off the stern into the warm salt water and swam lazily between the piers, avoiding the mats of floating seaweed, while the women sat on the afterdeck watching us. Thomas dove off the cockpit roof, stood on the edge with his back to the water and dove backward off the roof, turning a somersault in the air on his way down. He smashed the water, landing flat on his back, and disappeared between the

47

two great splashes that came up on each side of him as he went down.

"Ouch!" I said.

"Get hurt?" E. H. asked, when Thomas raised his head and blew.

"No. I'm used to a diving board. Didn't get the spring."

Thomas didn't try any more dives. He stayed in a long time after E. H. came out, and he and I were swimming alone together. He floated on his back with his nose and toes poking out, let the water run into his mouth and spouted like a whale.

"Ah, I love the water," he said.

"Fine place here, isn't it?"

"Swell. Ever seen the propellers under water?"

"No."

"Follow me."

At the stern of the *Pilar* Thomas inflated his chest with a deep breath and went down. I followed him under the boat to the big propeller with my eyes open in the salt water and saw his short legs ahead near the small blur of brass at the side. Then I had to come up for air. Thomas stayed under a while longer and came to the surface twenty feet from the boat, floating on his back, spouting and enjoying himself. I went out and he stayed in alone, swimming leisurely near the stern. E. H. stood on the fish box watching him. Suddenly Thomas's round face twisted in an expression of pain. He cried out, and E. H. dove in after him.

"Oh! I've lost my leg!" I thought I heard him say.

E. H. dove off the fish box and came up holding Thomas by the arm.

"It isn't of much value," Thomas said. "It's just one of those things a person gives you that you like to keep."

"What did you lose?" E. H. asked, letting go of Thomas's arm.

"A ring."

"Oh, I thought you said you'd lost your leg." E. H. said, swimming toward the boat, with John Charles Thomas following him on board.

"Did you say you thought I'd lost my leg?" Thomas asked.

"That's what I thought you said. That's why I dove in. I was going to help you out."

"Did you think I'd been struck by a barracuda?"

"I didn't know."

"Christ! You scared me."

"You scared me, too."

"I'm not going in here again."

"It's absolutely safe," E. H. said. "That was just a misunderstanding."

"Just the same, I'm not going in here again."

Thomas found his ring with his clothes where he had left it. We took off our wet trunks, rubbed ourselves dry with the rough white towels and dressed. As he was dressing, E. H. talked about his dive. "If you think a man is in danger, you act first," he said. "You find out later what the trouble is." Then they all piled into Hemingway's roadster and drove away to have dinner at his house.

6

A Help Problem

THE NEXT MORNING the Thomases were fishing guests. E. H. ran the *Pilar* over to the yacht and Thomas came on board with his wife, again wearing dark glasses and black bloomers, and Earl, the white man who had come on board the day before with the big Negro. Earl, a blond, sophisticated fellow, had been a Palm Beach fishing guide before Thomas made him captain of his yacht. As we headed south toward the Western Dry Rocks, Earl stood beside Hemingway at the wheel and they talked about the time of the biggest sailfish run at Palm Beach as compared with Key West and the marlin off Cuba.

It was a warm, cloudy day, and when we were out in the blue water of the Gulf Stream, trolling to eastward, the boat rolling in the heavy swells, Thomas went forward and lay down on his back on top of the round cabin roof with his hands folded across his chest; the tossing of the boat rocked him to sleep. His wife, fishing in the stern, could see him when she turned her head and looked through the cockpit windows, unless there were people standing by the wheel obstructing her view. Thomas was built so round he looked like he would roll off.

"Is he still there?" she would ask.

"He's all right," E. H. would answer. "He won't fall off."

"He's always doing that. He'll go to sleep anywhere. He makes me nervous."

Mrs. Thomas was young and slender, but with her dark glasses and black bloomers it was hard to tell whether she could be attractive. I sat beside her a long time, fishing the other rod, and she did not say anything. When the clouds finally split and the sun came out bright she was sitting on the port side with the sun hot in her face and I was in the shade.

"Let's change sides," I offered. "I'm used to the sun."

"No, I don't mind it," she answered, without taking her eyes off the trolled bait, as if she felt obliged to be civil but disliked talking with other people's servants and did not want me to speak to her again.

A few drops of rain fell and Thomas woke up and came astern, rubbing his eyes and yawning, looking fresh and cheerful after his sleep on the roof. He cleared his throat and asked, "Catch any fish?"

"A few bonito and mackerel. Nothing big," E. H. answered. "There's a fresh bait waiting for you."

"No, thanks. I like the water but I don't care to fish."

"Sing us a song," I said.

Thomas sang a funny little seaman's song in a soft whisper, complying with the request and making us laugh without showing off his voice.

"Sing us a louder one. You know, the kind where they beller."

"I don't feel like bellering now."

"How about a drink?" E. H. asked Thomas.

"I think it would be a very good idea."

"What will you have," I asked Thomas, "gin with lime and bitters?"

"Yes, and a little gin if you please."

"How many?" I asked E. H.

"Do you want one?" E. H. asked Earl.

"No, thanks."

"I'll have a whiskey," E. H. said, "with a little whiskey in it and mix one for yourself."

I mixed the drinks and sat down on the bunk beside Thomas, who sat with his stomach out a little, knees far apart and heels touching.

"Ah, this is a good dish. A very good dish," Thomas told his captain. "Better have one, Earl."

Earl shook his head.

"One won't hurt any."

"I'm off that stuff," Earl said.

"Strike!" Mrs. Thomas said.

E. H. shut down the motor, stopping the boat as Mrs. Thomas let the line out, and when she put on the drag and struck he raced the boat ahead to take the slack out of the line and we heard the scream of the reel as her rod whipped and the taut line jerked off into the water. This Thomas knew how to fish.

"Need any help?" Mr. Thomas asked his wife.

"What have you got?" E. H. asked her.

"It tapped like a sailfish."

"Funny it doesn't jump."

"Maybe she's got Lon Chaney down there," Thomas said. "You never can tell."

"Isn't Mister Thomas funny?" said Bumby, Hemingway's handsome ten-year-old son, who spent his winters in Chicago with his mother and his summers in Key West.

"He's very funny," E. H. answered his son.

"I don't know why Will Rogers and all those fellows should make so much money," Thomas said. "Can I help you, dear? She's on her good behavior now. You ought to hear her sometimes when I ask her that."

The bill and head and then the purple sail of a sailfish fighting on the surface rolled slowly out of the water, but the fish did not jump.

"Foul hooked!" E. H. said. "I saw blood. Work him in fast or the sharks'll get him."

"Oh, isn't that a shame!" Mrs. Thomas said, bracing her legs and fighting the fish as hard as she was able.

"Need any help?" chirped John Thomas, slapping his knees.

"Tell me how you want the boat," E. H. said. "I can run up on him if you want me to."

"No, I've still got line."

"You're tired, dear," Thomas told his struggling wife. "Take it easy. You'd better rest awhile. Let somebody else take it."

"I'll bet it gets away," Hank whispered.

"Don't mouth the fish," E. H. said sharply.

Mrs. Thomas worked the fish toward the boat inch by inch, so slowly we expected to see a shark come up from the rear and bite its tail off. It must have taken her thirty minutes to bring the fish to the stern. She led it alongside the boat and Earl, acting now in an official capacity, reached down over the side with a handkerchief covering his hand and grabbed the sailfish's spear; when it pulled away he did not try to hold it with the leader, but waited until she led the fish alongside again and the next time he got a good hold of the skin, clubbed him over the eyes and pulled him on board without a mark on him.

"Nice work," E. H. said. "Did you see how he did that? It's a good system. That way you don't lose so many fish at the boat. Congratulations, Mrs. Thomas. You fought him very well. He's foul-hooked right in back of the gill plate. That's why it pulled so hard. It pulled like a bucket. Let's have a drink on that. Are you sure you don't want one, Earl?"

"No thanks, Ernest."

"Go ahead, Earl," Thomas said.

Earl shook his head, but when I went below to mix the drinks he followed me into the galley and whispered, "Mix me one, too. I'll drink it here. Don't tell anyone."

We ran in early and tied alongside Thomas's yacht, the others going on board and Earl staying with me to help fix the malfunctioning water pump in the galley, and while we took the pump apart he told me to mix him a gin drink. The big Negro was standing by listening when the engineer asked Earl how he liked Hemingway.

"He's a hell of a swell fellow," Earl said. "I started calling him Mister Hemingway and he says, 'My name is Ernest.' "

"Mr. Thomas looks like a good fellow to work for," I said.

"He is. They're swell people. Sometimes he gets a little funny, though, and I'd just as soon tell him to go to hell as not."

Earl fitted a new piece of leather into the pump and had another drink, which he emptied half finished when E. H. and Pauline came, and then he left.

"We'll go over and weigh your fish," E. H. told Mrs. Thomas.

"I'll mix the drinks by the time you get back," Thomas said.

We ran over to the Thompson dock and put the sailfish on ice in the ice plant. When we returned to the yacht, Thomas was not in sight but some of his crew and the Negro stood at the rail waiting for us to throw the ropes. I threw the bowline to the engineer and I heard the Negro astern say, "Throw it here, Ernest."

"Mister Hemingway to you."

"Yes, sir."

"You needn't get too niggerish. You're not that far south yet."
The black man was silent.

John Charles Thomas came out of a cabin door wearing a black
suit, a white shirt and a big black bowtie, walking toward us with
his chest out and his head back as he might walk out on a stage
in an auditorium full of people. For a moment I expected to hear
him burst into a song, but he didn't. He was all set now to become
an impressive host and it was obvious he had spent his time dressing
and not in mixing drinks.

"Come on board and we'll have a drink," he said.

"Thanks. We haven't time unless you've got one ready," E. H.
answered. "We came back to tell you the fish weighed sixty-four
pounds."

"Thanks. It won't take long. Better come up and have one."

"It's getting late. We'll have to get back. Pull in the bowline,
Arnold."

"We wish you could stay," Mrs. Thomas said. "Thanks for telling
us about the fish and thanks for a lovely time."

"It's in the ice plant if you want it mounted."

"No, I don't think so," Thomas said. "Sorry you can't stay for a
drink."

Thomas was left dressed up without any company when E. H.
headed the *Pilar* into the setting sun toward the naval yard. The
people on the yacht were watching us and we did not talk until
we were far enough away so that they could not hear what we
said. Hank was sitting on the fish box and I stood near E. H., who
was at the wheel with Pauline beside him.

"Wasn't that Negro awful?" she said. "I'm glad you snubbed him
the way you did."

"There was nothing personal about it," E. H. told me. "I was
just planing him down like a carpenter planes a rough board."

"I can't understand why Thomas keeps him," Pauline said.

"He only hired him a couple days ago."

"He isn't a bit like our jigs. We've got nice jigs, haven't we?"

"He probably got that way fishing with drunks in Bimini, and
now when a man has a few drinks he thinks he can say what he
likes."

"He was on board yesterday," I said. "I thought he was pretty
arrogant. He went down through the cabins putting his hands

on the walls and nosing into everything without being invited."

"I hope you snubbed him good," Pauline said.

"I felt like it but I didn't know if I should. How do you like the Thomases?"

"They're nice people," E. H. said.

"You could sure tell she was born rich," I said, thinking of the time I offered to change places with her.

"Was she?" Pauline asked Ernest.

"Yes," he said.

"Now tell me, Arnold, how could you tell she was born wealthy? I couldn't."

"It's just the way she acted."

"How could Arnold tell?" she asked E. H. "I couldn't see anything different about her."

"I told you he was good," E. H. said. "Arnold Samuelson! The coming American novelist!"

"Do you think I had wealthy parents?" Pauline asked me.

"No."

"But they were, quite wealthy."

"Well, you're different. You went out and worked."

"Yes, you lost that, Mummy," E. H. said.

"But I can't understand how you could tell she was wealthy. It's a mystery to me. It seems I can't tell anything about people."

"Sure you can, Mummy," E. H. said. "You threw away a novel that was better than *Main Street.*"

"Could I write as good as Sinclair Lewis?"

"Much better."

"Could I write as good as Ernest Hemingway?"

"Now, don't start that, Mummy."

"But I want to know how Arnold could tell. Did you notice anything about Mrs. Thomas, Leicester?"

"Yes. I sort of thought she was born rich," Hank said from the fish box, taking all the glory away from me.

"How could you tell?"

"I don't know. She just gave me that impression. I can't explain why."

"There, you see, both of these young fellows knew it and I never noticed a thing."

"I'll tell you how they knew," E. H. said. "I told both of them this morning. No singer alive could pay for a boat like that."

When E. H. drove his roadster out on the pier the next morning, there was no block of ice on the bumper and I knew he had only come down to look the boat over and we were not going fishing. He said "Good morning" sitting in the car and I answered standing on the fish box.

"Thomas's yacht pulled out a while ago," I said. "Thomas came over in the motor boat to get a cookie jar they left on board."

"Did he look like something was the matter?"

"He didn't look very cheerful. Looked like he had a hangover."

"They had a hell of a time last night. Earl got drunk and fired the nigger and Thomas fired Earl."

"I gave Earl a few drinks when he was fixing the pump."

"So that's when he started. He must have got some more downtown. I tried to talk Thomas out of firing him. The boat was at anchor, so it didn't matter if he did get drunk. You heard Thomas encouraging him to take a drink. If I'd known he was a rummy, I'd never have tried to get him started."

"Earl told me he might tell Thomas to go to hell."

"Maybe he did. Maybe that's what made Thomas sore. He said he couldn't keep a captain that got drunk. It's too bad. Earl was with him two years and they thought the world of him. Thomas was looking all over town last night trying to find another captain. He must have found one if he's pulled out."

"Too bad about Earl."

"Yes. He's a damned good fellow. He maybe wasn't a very good captain because he didn't know how to keep discipline, but he knew his stuff about fishing."

"Wonder what he'll do now."

"Probably go back to taking out farmers at Palm Beach."

E. H. invited me up to the house for supper that evening.

"We live well," Pauline remarked.

"We work well, too," E. H. said. "I had a funny dream last night. I dreamt I had a fight with Gene Tunney. He had me down choking the life out of me and I kicked him in the groin."

"You shouldn't have done that, even in a dream."

"I'm a realist, Mummy."

7

The Telegram

HANK AND JIM received their clearance papers for Havana and their boat had been dry-docked and repainted and was all set to sail, but they never quite got ready to leave. They had been in Key West a month, living on Hemingway's yacht and going out fishing with him every day, and they seemed to like that better than risking their lives in the seventeen-foot boat, which was so small that light winds raised great storms at sea when they were sailing in it and the next wave always seemed worth another prayer.

Hank had been seasick every rough day we went out into the stream, and he realized the storms he had survived in the Gulf of Mexico were calms compared with ordinary sailing weather in the Gulf Stream. If he got seasick on the *Pilar,* what would it be like in his little tub with its prow built so high they could not sail against the wind, only with it, and the stern cockpit so low the water splashed in?

Hank had spent six months and six hundred dollars building the *Hawkshaw,* and he had been a year planning and talking about the trip. If he gave up now and abandoned his boat in Key West, Captain Bra told him he would be lucky to get ten dollars for it.

"I'd give you five dollars for your boat," Bra offered. "Not because I'd ever have any use for it or think it's worth five dollars, but I'd pay that much just so you wouldn't go down to a watery grave. That's where you'll end up if you start out from here."

"She cost me six hundred besides all the work," replied Hank, who said he had prayed many times on the trip from Mobile but would not admit he was afraid to cross the Gulf Stream.

"You can pick up better boats than that in Key West for ten dollars. Lots of them."

"She's got good lines. A yachtsman designed her for me."

"She looks more like a grouper."

"But she's a good sea boat."

"She hasn't sunk yet, but she will. It wouldn't take much of a wave to tip her over. She's too small and she's top heavy."

"Just the same, she's built strong. I know because I built her myself."

One day, while I was exercising in the quiet water of the navy yard, I saw the *Hawkshaw's* wooden rudder come loose and drift away. Hank spent a day putting it back and repairing the broken part. He had to admit it was a good thing the rudder came off when it did rather than halfway across the Gulf Stream.

E. H. gave Hank the maps he needed, and told him that if he intended to go to South America he ought to start soon, because from Key West to Cuba was his longest and most dangerous trip out of sight of land and he ought to be alongside the islands, where he could go in at the first sign of a storm before the midsummer hurricane season.

"I'm not afraid of hurricanes," Hank said.

"That's because you've never seen one. If you got in a hurricane, you wouldn't have a chance. It would pick you right up out of the sea."

"I'm not afraid, anyway."

"How about you, Jim, are you afraid of hurricanes?"

"No, I don't think so," Jim said.

Hank finally decided to leave, and one morning while they were making ready E. H. drove out on the pier.

"I've got some bad news for you, Jim," he said, watching Jim carefully.

"What's that?"

"You got a telegram this morning. I opened it because I knew it might be something important. It says your mother's sick. They want you to come home at once."

Jim bit his lower lip and looked down at the deck, while E. H., standing above on the pier, watched his face.

"I suppose I'll have to go, then," Jim said.

"We can telegraph your mother's doctor and find out how serious it is. I'll pay for the telegrams."

Jim did not answer.

"Gosh, that's too bad, Jim," Hank said. "I'm awfully sorry."

"She might not be as bad as they think," E. H. said. "It wouldn't take long to telegraph the doctor."

"If they sent for me, I suppose I'll have to go."

"I'm awfully sorry, Jim," Hank said again. "It's too bad we have to give up the trip together after we'd planned on it so long."

"I'm sorry, too."

"They might send another telegram," E. H. said. "Come with me up to the house and we'll wait for it there. Then you'll find out as soon as it gets here."

The two young shipmates rode to the house in Hemingway's car and I did not see them again until late in the afternoon, when Jim came on board with Hank to pack his clothes and get ready for the six o'clock train to Miami. I saw Hank give Jim the money he needed for a railroad ticket to his home in Michigan.

"I know you'd do the same for me if I needed it," Hank told him. "It's too bad this happened now, when we were all set to leave. I'd hate to give up the trip, Jim. You be sure to write to me, Jim, and if your mother gets better, maybe we can make the trip anyway."

"Yes, I'll do that. Are you sure you won't need this money?"

"No. I don't need it because I can't make the trip anyway now until I get somebody else. Go ahead."

"Well, thanks, pal."

"There's Ernest's car."

Hemingway took them to the train, where they said goodbye, and Hank was left stranded in Key West, a captain with a boat but no crew.

"Jim was spooked! Absolutely spooked!" E. H. said to Captain Bra. "I knew it the minute I got the telegram. That's why I tried to get him to send a telegram to his mother's doctor to find out how sick she was. I offered to pay for it several times, but he wouldn't bother and then I knew for sure he was spooked. I had been waiting for him to do that because it was his only easy way out. When they saw those waves out in the stream they saw something different, and she's ninety miles across. It was all right as long as they stayed on board here, going out fishing every day and living good, then they liked it fine, but when I talked them into leaving next week Jim wrote a letter home and asked them to send a telegram. It was very easy."

"Does Hank know about it?"

"No. Hank thinks Jim is a gentleman."

"I saw Hank give Jim money for his fare home," I said.

"Jim is probably the better businessman."

"What will Hank do now?"

"He'll stay here till he gets somebody else."

"He won't get anybody from Key West," Captain Bra said. "These Conchs knows too much about boats."

8

The World's Toughest Racket

"How MANY WORDS do you write a day?" I asked E. H. one afternoon out in the stream.

"That varies," he answered. "Sometimes you can write a lot and some days you can't write."

"Bernard Shaw says if a man wants to be a writer he ought to write at least a thousand words every day."

"That's too much. A thousand words is a hell of a good day's work. If you kept that up, you'd pump yourself dry and you'd just write shit. If you wrote five hundred words a day, there's no publisher who could publish all your stuff. That would be a hundred and eighty thousand words or two novels a year. Have you ever tried any of those exercises we talked about?"

"No. I want to write, but every time I try I have the feeling I can't do it."

"That doesn't mean anything. I feel absolutely impotent every time I sit down to write. Writing is hard work. It's the hardest work in the world. It is the world's toughest racket. If it was easy, everybody would be doing it. All they'd have to do would be to sit down and write a story and send it off and get a check back. The only reason they pay good money is there aren't many people who can do it."

"What is the best way to make a story interesting?"

"Anybody can write an exciting story and make it interesting.

The trick is to learn how to write a quiet story and make it interesting. If you can do that, you won't have any trouble when you get an exciting story."

"Are the best stories based on personal experience?"

"No, the best stories are invented. You've got to invent the action. In real life, only one out of ten people ever have anything happen to them that would make a story. If you write about yourself, you die one time and you're through. If you write about others, you can die a thousand deaths and keep on writing. You can take a person you know, you can change his age and his background and put him in a country he has never seen and he is still a true person. You put him in an interesting situation and you invent the action. When you learn to invent you can write any number of stories.

"If you think you've got a good story, go ahead and write it and get it off your chest. That's the kind you can write at one sitting. I remember one time I wrote two stories in one day. I wrote one and when I got through, I was still feeling good and I wrote another one.

"When you write a story like that, put it away for a couple of weeks and when you read it you get the reader's point of view. If you didn't think it was any good, you wouldn't be writing it. You can't tell until you write it and put it away and then go back to it with a reader's point of view and you see what you've got."

"I read 'The Killers' again. That's a swell story."

"Yes. They make them read that at the colleges."

"I read it when I was taking English but I'd forgotten you wrote it. It's one of the best you've ever written, isn't it?"

"It has something of the fourth dimension. It comes close to a man's soul and that's the most difficult thing there is to do. I'd rather not take the easy shots if I stand a chance to make a hard one."

"I wish I could learn to write."

"You've got a chance. Anybody's got a chance if he sets out to be the greatest writer that ever lived. One thing I have done is open the gates of literature to any man who has a good story. No matter how he writes it, if it's good, he can find a publisher."

"Have you always wanted to write?"

"Yes. What you want to do now is learn to use your eyes and see things as they actually happen, so when you write you can present them just as they are. You want to be careful about comparing a thing with something else, because a thing isn't like anything else. It is itself. I won't try to teach you to write like I do. There is such a thing as absolute writing, and if I can teach you that, you can develop your own style afterward."

"Would you mind if I tried to write an article about fishing for a sports magazine?"

"Go ahead and write it. Then I'll go over your stuff and help you all I can. I've got a picture of the record sailfish you can have to send in. We should be able to fix up something they'll take."

That afternoon I felt a very light tap, as if my bait had caught in a small seaweed, and I clicked off line to the count of ten as I had been told to do whenever I felt anything I wasn't sure of and then set the drag, intending to reel in and pick off the weed, but the line suddenly became alive, racing off the spool, bending and jerking the rod, and a sailfish with his purple sail stretched erect from his back reared up on his tail and flung himself clear out of the sea, hitting the water again with a splash and jumping three more times before he went off on another run. A jumping sailfish when he is on your line is a much more interesting spectacle than one somebody else is fishing, and you feel altogether differently about the sport. Keeping the line taut, I turned him and began working him in. In ten minutes my first sailfish was on board.

"You fought him well," E. H. said.

"I've known fellows who've spent thousands of dollars trying to catch one of them," Bra said. "There's one fellow who has been down here in his yacht every year for the last twelve years and he hasn't caught one yet. His guests have but he hasn't."

We hung up the sailfish flag, and when we came in Pauline was at the dock.

"Who caught the fish?" she asked.

"Arnold," E. H. said.

"Wonderful! I might have known. So that's the reason you're looking so happy."

The real reason I looked so happy was that E. H. had said I could write an article about fishing with him. I spent the next ten days writing and rewriting a fishing piece, and when I had it worked over so many times that every line and every word had become set and I could do nothing more with it I gave the twelve pages to E. H. and he took the manuscript up to his workshop. A few minutes later he called me from his window and told me to come up. When I came in he was seated at his desk writing with a pencil on one of the pages.

"I've been going over your piece. It's interesting but there are too damned many Ernests in it." he said.

"I was wondering what to call you," I replied, very ill at ease. "I thought it would sound awkward to call you Mister Hemingway all the time."

"Of course. But you know how it would be yourself if I wrote a piece about you and called you Arnold, Arnold, Arnold, Arnold, Arnold, Arnold, Arnold."

I nodded.

"There are a few inaccuracies. I'll try to fix it up and eliminate some of the Ernests. You don't mind if I do this, do you?"

"Oh, no!"

"Then I'll see you when I've finished."

An hour later he came down the outside stairway and across the lawn to the coon cage I was building for his pet coons under the sapodilla tree, with the pages in his hand, smiling and evidently feeling good.

"I went over your piece," he said.

"Were you disappointed?"

"Not at all. It's three hundred percent better than the newspaper stuff you showed me about bumming. There's no comparison. Then I wasn't so sure whether you could ever make a writer, but now I see you might stand a chance.

"Here are some corrections," he said, showing me the places on the first page where he had written in pencil in the margins and between the typewritten lines. "I'm not trying to make you write the way I do. I can imitate anybody, and what I added I wrote just as you might have written it yourself and you'll begin to believe you wrote the whole thing yourself after you've typed it and read it over a few times. One criticism is that that there is too much Hemingway and not enough fish. Here, when you were writing about the first time you called on me, you said, 'It was fortunate that I came in the afternoon,' and I added, 'If it had been in the morning, I believe I might have been thrown out.' That's the truth and the truth is always interesting. I had to put that in or the readers would think, well, all we've got to do is to meet this guy Hemingway and we'll be all set. All the bums in the country would be down here. You see I've got rid of most of the Ernests, scratching some out and substituting E. H., which is better. Your paragraphs are too short. They'd look choppy on a printed page, and your sentences are too short. There are times when you can use short sentences, but you've got to learn when, because if you use them too much you get a monotonous trip-hammer action that tires the reader. Another thing I noticed from what you said about the priest is you have a tendency to condemn before you completely understand. You'll have to watch that. You aren't God and you never judge a man. You present him as he is and you let the reader judge. A writer has to be made up of two different persons. As a man you can be any kind of a son of a bitch you like, you can hate and condemn a person and shoot his head off the next time you see him, but as a writer you have got to see him absolutely as he is, you've got to understand his viewpoint completely and learn how to present him accurately without getting your own reactions mixed up in it before you can write about him. Some of the things you said about the priest weren't true. He really is a good fisherman and he held on till his back gave out. After all, he's a friend of mine, but I suppose I liked him better than you did."

E. H. handed me the manuscript.

"Is it worth doing anything with?"

"Sure. There might be a chance. Type it over and send it off. The worst they can do is send it back. If they don't take it, don't get discouraged. You'll get something better later on."

"Thanks very much."

"Not at all. The reason I read it right away was I knew you might be anxious to find out about it and I was glad to do it when I saw you were getting better. You ought to see some of the stories people send to have me read. Some day I'll show you some of them."

"Do you really think I might make a writer?"

"Your chances look better than they did. Much better. What you want to work on now is your sentences and try to learn how to build up a paragraph. You'll see how I've run them together and you'll get the idea."

"I'm sorry it took up so much of your time when you could have been working."

"That's all right. If you had tried to show me something the first day you came I might not have taken the trouble, but now that I know you I'm glad to do it."

"Well, thanks very much."

"Not at all."

9

Havana

E. H. WAS LIKE a father to me. He treated me like one of the family
and in return I tried to keep the boat in shape. Although that
was what he was paying me for, he was grateful for everything I
did. It was the first time in my life that I was completely happy
when I had a job, and the only thing I worried about was losing
it. He never said anything about not taking me along to Cuba and
I assumed he would but was afraid he might change his mind. He
had planned to leave in late May so as to be in Havana in time
for the first of the marlin run and fish it through to the end of
the season in the fall, but when the time came to go he received
word that the marlin had not yet been sighted by Havana fishermen
and he postponed the trip to wait for better reports, being well
along in his story and going good, and he thought it would be more
profitable to write in Key West than loaf in Havana until the fish
came. We waited another month, fishing sailfish in the Gulf Stream,
and in the middle of July, Carlos Gutiérrez, his Cuban boatman,
wrote that the marlin had begun running and that Woodward, an
American living in Havana, had hooked into a doubleheader, both
big marlin and both getting away.

We began to get ready the day the news came. E. H. applied
for clearance papers, signing himself on the crew list as captain
and me as first engineer, as we were permitted to carry more guns
and ammunition when we went as officers. We had already stowed
half a truckload of canned food on board, and all there was left
to do was to run the *Pilar* over to the Thompson dock and fill
her gasoline tanks. In the evening, E. H. brought down his rumble
seat full of heavy fishing tackle, eighteen-ounce Hardy rods; big
5° Hardy reels; thirty-two-thread line, 500 yards to the spool, and
enough pfleuger hoods and heavy piano-wire leaders for several
seasons. Then we were ready to leave, there was no doubt of my
going along, and I stayed awake most of the night thinking of how
it would be over there in Havana, having Cubans doing all the

work and me a guest, fishing big fish with Hemingway in the daytime and seeing the sights of Havana at night.

E. H. had said "You haven't seen anything yet."

On the morning of July 18, I heard the cars come out on the dock before sunrise, when it was getting gray in the east over town and a cool breeze was coming off the reef after a hot night. The boat being tied to both piers, lying out of reach between them, I slacked a few yards off the bowline and pulled the stern into the pier, making her fast when the rudder touched. E. H. was on the dock with Pauline and several friends who had got up early to see us off. He handed me heavy fishing reels, marlin-size rods, tuna gut, guns in sheepskin cases, clothes and boxes of hooks and leads.

"Well, Ernest, I hope you get that big marlin you're after," Sully, the boilermaker, said.

"Thanks, Sully."

"I hope he beats Zane Grey."*

"You want to watch out for those hot Spanish señoritas," old Captain Bra told me. "Three ways! *Tres veces.*" He held up three fingers.

"Tell them hello for me," he said. "There are some good-looking ones over there. I wish I was going along."

"You'll be over later on, won't you?"

"I'd like to, but my old woman wouldn't stand for it."

Captain Bra had had one hell of a time last year. E. H. doctored his penis every night. One woman kept coming down to the boat and had him convinced she was in love with him three ways and that she wanted to marry him. Mrs. Bra wanted no more of that.

We had to wait a few minutes for Charles Lund, the navigator E. H. had hired to steer us across. He came at daybreak, slim and smiling and apologizing for being late. E. H. started both motors, and the people on the dock cast off the lines and stood waving at us until we were out of sight on the other side of the breakwater.

E. H. and Lund changed off at the wheel, steering a southward course to the left of Sand Key. The buildings of Key West disappeared behind our wake, in an hour we had dropped the radio towers and in another hour the Sand Key lighthouse, and all we could

---

* Zane Grey (1875–1939), known primarily for his Western stories, had recently authored two highly successful books on big-game fishing, *Tales of Fishing* and *Tales of Swordfish and Tuna.*

see was water. I opened three bottles of beer and E. H. and Lund threw the empties over for target practice with the .22 Colt automatic. It was too rough to hit a target tossing on the waves and the boat rolled so much I began to feel like not eating and lay on my back on the bunk opposite the wheel most of the time, listening to Lund and E. H. talk. E. H. was watching for flying fish and birds, and Lund, standing at the wheel with his feet far apart, said he was used to the slow motion of the Havana–Key West ferry. He was getting a kick out of taking the cruiser across. They were enjoying the trip, E. H. as a fisherman exploring untried fishing grounds, and Lund as a boatman. I was the seasick passenger waiting for land.

"Do you like the sea?" I asked Lund.

"Hell, yes," he said. "If I wasn't married I'd travel all over the damned world."

"How do you like it on the ferry?"

"Too much the same thing all the time. I wouldn't have taken the job if it wasn't for my wife."

"Have you ever tried to get a job as captain of a yacht?" E. H. asked him.

"No."

"Now that you're married, I think you'd like that. You get along well with people and the yacht owners would make a God of you. They always do. Their captain is the God they've made with their own money, they're proud of him and they treat him like a king. If you got in with a rich bastard, he might stay in one port six months at a time and you'd be home every night."

"I'd like to take a shot at it."

"If you met the right people, you'd be all set."

Flying fish sailed out of the water away from both sides of the boat and more kept shooting out in thick droves as we passed over their grounds.

"Look at them! Look at them!" E. H. said. "There must be fish out here. You know what? Sometime it would be fun to take the boat out to the middle of the stream. We could fish all day and drift all night. It would be fun just to see what we'd catch. It might be bloody marvelous fishing out here. What do you think?"

"It might," Lund answered, having crossed the stream almost every day for years. "Funny, I never thought of it before."

"In the morning when we wanted to go back we could take our

bearings and run in. There must be fish here. Let's get a feather out."

E. H. trolled a feather for a while, but the boat was going too fast and he reeled in.

Lund knew when the mountains would appear early in the afternoon if the boat was averaging ten knots and the course was true, and when the time came, E. H., standing in the bow looking ahead through his field glasses, saw them first because he was up higher.

"Exactly where they should be," Lund said, proud of his navigation. "Havana is dead ahead."

"Are they near Havana?" I asked E. H.

"Thirty miles up the coast," he answered. "They're the mountains of Cabañas."

"Will we ever see them up close?"

"When Pauline comes over. We'll take a trip up the coast and stay overnight in Cabañas harbor."

"I'd like to see some mountains again."

"They're not very rough. Nothing like the Rockies."

By afternoon, the tiny round tops of the mountains had risen higher and wider, and spread out in a blue ridge above the sea, and then, toward sundown, the long flat line of the Cuban coast came into sight, turning from blue to a dark green as we approached at an angle, the grayish buildings of Havana looking like a small town.

"Think we'll make her in time to clear?" E. H. asked.

"Think we will," Lund replied, pushing the gasoline levers ahead and racing the motors.

"Better take her easy and be sure of getting in."

Lund left the motors racing because he wanted to spend the night ashore in Havana and he knew after six o'clock we would be too late to clear and nobody could leave the ship until morning. E. H. was afraid the motors were being pushed too hard, but he said nothing more about it.

"I smell something," I said, being seasick and sensitive to smells.

"Something's burning!" E. H. said. "Take a look in the galley."

The odor of burning grew stronger and stronger, but we could not locate the fire. We looked everywhere, with the growing, tense excitement known only to passengers on burning ships. E. H. opened the doors above the engine pit and found the big motor so hot the paint was frying off the cylinder head, causing the smell. The pump that circulated water to cool the motor had stopped pumping, and we had to turn the motor off and try to run in on the 40 h.p. Lycoming, which E. H. had had installed for such emergencies.

The Morro Castle was only three miles ahead and we would have arrived in twenty more minutes at the usual cruising speed, but with the small motor barely able to hold the boat against the current of the Gulf Stream, we crawled along slowly for two hours and entered the harbor between the stone wall of Morro Castle and the low Havana waterfront at twilight. A launch filled with soldiers in khaki came out to meet us, and ran alongside, a soldier standing with his rifle at parade dress in the bow asking E. H. questions in Spanish. The guards on the lookout tower of the Morro Castle had seen the *Pilar* approach at a good speed until within three miles of land at sundown and then it had stopped and approached slowly, acting as if she might be loaded with contraband ammunition for the revolutionaries, afraid to come in before dark. They had sent the soldiers to search the ship. E. H. told the soldiers he was an American yachtsman and fisherman and had come to Havana to fish marlin, and the soldiers replied it was a good story but they had to search the boat anyhow. They were ready to come on board and search when another launch approached and an excited voice shouted, *"¡El Hemingway!"*

"¡Qué tal, Carlos!" E. H. greeted his boatman.

The soldiers became polite and apologetic when they heard that name. They knew Hemingway as the American millionaire who the summer before had caught sixty-four marlin with rod and reel and had given away tons of marlin meat to the natives on the dock. They said they had not recognized him in his new yacht, they were sorry they had made the mistake, they hoped he would catch many marlin again this year and they went away.

The water in the Havana harbor was calm and restful, and everything was new and interesting. We ran in through the channel, past the fishing smacks along the fortress and the ocean boulevard on the Havana side. The channel widened and E. H. stopped near the pier the fishing smacks used to unload their fish. Lund threw the big anchor off the bow and when it took a hold in the mud, he hitched the rope to the bitt. The incident with the soldiers was over and now when we lay at anchor and had to stay there all night we had time to think about the big motor having broken down. We did not know how long we would be delayed until it could be fixed, or whether E. H. would have to send to the factory for new parts or whether there were mechanics in Havana who could fix it or what the cost might be, and Lund was blaming himself for having run the motors too fast and E. H. might have been silently agreeing with him, although neither of them mentioned it while they talked of other things.

It would have cost $25 extra to clear after six o'clock. E. H. offered to clear if Lund wanted to go uptown to Havana, but he turned the offer down. They talked in the cabin until bedtime and then we all slept on board.

When the customs officers came on board in the morning, they seemed interested only in the way the boat was built, with sleeping accommodations for six people below and a galley and a john and everything, and they didn't try to find hidden ammunition. They opened a few locker drawers as they passed through the cabins without unpacking anything or finding the rifles concealed behind the bunks. E. H. could have had a ton of dynamite under the cockpit deck without it being discovered. The doctor glanced at us and we took down the yellow quarantine flag.

Carlos, the fifty-six-year-old Cuban, wearing a new white outfit with an officer's cap and the letters PILAR sewed across his chest, was standing by in a rowboat with the name *Bumby* painted on its side. When the yellow flag came down, he climbed on board, shook hands with E. H., his black eyes glistening with emotion, and talked excitedly in Spanish, finding the mop and mopping the deck as he talked. There had never been any deck-mopping in Key West. While I watched him mop the deck, I began to lose the comfortable feeling of being useful. I felt the uneasiness of a guest when he sees work being done and wonders whether he ought to help and feels in the way doing nothing. Carlos was getting the attention E. H. had given me when I was his boatman in Key West and E. H., besides being busy with other matters, seemed more reserved; he was now the captain of his ship, an army officer again, and our relationship was becoming less personal because we were on a long expedition together and he had to have discipline.

E. H. went ashore to send a telegram to Pauline, Carlos went along to help find a mechanic and Charles Lund was in a hurry to get on the ferry, leaving me alone on board.

"Don't worry, you'll see plenty of Havana," E. H. said. "You're not in the navy and you won't be seeing the world through a porthole."

I didn't mind being alone. There was plenty to look at. There was the immense stone wall of the old fortress, running all the way along the narrow channel to the turret of Morro Castle at the point of the harbor entrance, old and gray-looking in the early morning sunlight. There were the passenger boats and freighters from all over the world occasionally coming in and going out of the harbor, seeming to move very slowly because they were so big and leaving a swell that rocked the *Pilar* violently for several minutes after they had passed, and there were many smaller boats— motor launches filled with Cubans, and small, slow-moving rowboats with canvas tops over the stern to shade passengers while the oarsman sat toward the bow, rowing backward in the hot sun. On the Havana side, there were the dark faces and white suits of Cubans riding past the gray apartment buildings in small street cars and open automobiles on the waterfront boulevard. There were other Cubans, whose clothes were not so white, standing on the dock nearby, watching men whirl baited handlines around their fingers without having a bite, then throwing the untouched bait far out again.

An old rowboat came toward me and the Cuban in it, wearing more patches than pieces of his original shirt, pointed at the pineapples, grapefruit and bananas in the bow.

"No speak Spanish," I said.

"Ho Kay," he answered, waving his hands. "Me speak English. Want this? Want this? Want this?"

"How much pineapples?"

"How many want? One five cent. Two ten cent."

"Two," I said, handing him a dime.

"Want wine?" he asked, holding up a quart bottle.

"How much?"

"Forty cent."

"No, that's all."

"You have American cigarette, no?"

"Yes."

"Trade. Wine, one package American cigarette."

"Against the law."

"Me no speak," he said, shaking his head.

"Sorry."

"Two bottles wine, one package cigarette."

"No can do."

"One other day, more pineapple?"

"Sure, come back again."

When I told E. H. about it, he said, "Don't trust anybody. That fellow might have been a government spy trying to get you in bad. You can never tell who they are."

E. H. had returned with several Cubans, all gesturing freely with their arms and shoulders and speaking excitedly as if they were plotting a new revolution, and E. H., now that he was in Cuba where it was the custom of the country, talked as loudly and gestured as much as anybody. It was fun watching them talk, although I couldn't make anything out of it except that the water pump of the big motor was causing all the excitement and the rotund man named Cojo who walked on his heels was the mechanic who had come to find out why it did not work. Cojo took the pump apart and told E. H. the metal was burned out and the brass would have to be replaced. He knew metal workers in Havana who could do it, the motor would be as good as new the next morning and it would cost less than if E. H. were in the United States and had to send to the Chrysler factory for a new pump. That was wonderful news. It made everybody happy again, and from then on Cojo was our best friend and the most welcomed guest on board the ship. He was welcome to come along fishing every day and drink himself drunk on good whiskey every night if he wanted to.

In the evening, E. H. was preparing to meet Pauline on board the ferry. He had hired a young Spaniard named Juan who was recommended by the pilots as a good cook, and he left us with this admonition:

"We'll be staying at the Ambos Mundos, so I'll leave you and Juan to watch the ship tonight. Sleep light and if you hear anything get up and see what it is. You've heard us talk about the *Terribles Reglanos*. They're a gang of professional pirates living in Regla, that town over there, and they make their living stealing off American yachts anchored in the harbor. They come across the harbor in the night and they don't make any noise so you've got to be ready for them when they come. You sleep up forward with the pistol under your pillow. They might climb the anchor rope and try the forward hatch. Juan will sleep in the stern with the club.

If they come aboard stern first, he'll yell and wake you up, then he'll start clubbing them over the heads till you can get out with the pistol. You'll be down below, so you'll be able to see them and they won't be able to see you. Don't shoot to kill unless you have to. Try to shoot them in the legs but be careful not to shoot any holes in the ship."

"I see. I'll shoot at their knees first, and if they keep coming, I'll raise."

"Chances are the first shot will scare them away because we're so close to the dock, but be sure you've got a full clip."

"It's loaded."

"The moon will be out so they probably won't come tonight, but it's always best not to take chances. How do you sleep?"

"Like a log."

"You can train yourself to sleep light. Even if you don't hear anything, make a practice of getting up a few times in the night anyway and look around to see that everything is all right."

"Okay."

"Is there anything you need on shore?"

"No."

"Then Juan will row me ashore and I'll see you in the morning. Good night."

"Buenos notches."

"That's it. Pick up all the Spanish you can. Juan will make you a good tutor. He speaks pure Spanish."

Juan, hungry-looking, with high cheekbones, hollow cheeks and shoes that were cracked open, was thirty years old. He was a fiery talker, proud because he was a Spaniard and talked like one and not like a Cuban. He had come over from Spain when he was eighteen, and cooked on Cuban fishing smacks several years, staying out weeks at a time with no protection against hurricanes. During his last bad storm, he made up his mind that if he ever got out of it alive he would starve to death on land before he would ever go to sea again. When E. H. hired him, he was almost starved, not having had any work for two years. Now he found himself suddenly prosperous, having a job that paid twenty dollars a month and his board, good wages in Cuba, and that night, as we sat together on the afterdeck, he tried to start a conversation.

"Yo Juan," he said, pointing at himself. Then he pointed at me, *"Usted?"*

"Arnold."

"*¿Cómo?*"

"Arnold."

"Arnold, Engleesh, *muy bien,*" he said, nodding his head. *"Pero en español,* Arnold, no. *Es Arnoldo!"*

"Juan, Spaneesh, very good," I replied. "But in English, Juan, no. It's applesauce."

"¿Cómo?"

"Applesauce." Juan had never known that his name could be changed so much when translated into good English, and he tried to learn to pronounce the word "applesauce" so he could remember it and tell his friends. He was an enthusiastic teacher and scholar, and traded English for Spanish, pointing at the water, the boats, streetcars, automobiles, the moon and the stars and everything else we could see, each giving the names for them as spoken in his own country, soon forgetting the words of the other language and having to point at them again, repeating the words until we could remember some of them, and when we decided to go to bed, Juan appeared well satisfied with our progress.

"Pronto Arnoldo speaka *español,* Juan speaka Engleesh," he said.

"Watch out for the *Terribles Reglanos.*"

Juan grinned and flourished the club. Hearing the word *"Terribles,"* he knew what I meant.

The *Terribles* did not come that night. At sunrise, I awoke hearing Carlos, barefooted on the cabin roof, mopping the dew off the painted canvas as I used to do in Key West every morning. I went to sleep again and slept until the sun was high enough to come down on me through the forward hatch and the heat made me feel like getting up. Juan was ashore buying food at the market and Carlos, having raised the American flag and cleaned up the ship, was sitting in the stern oiling the big fishing reels. At eight o'clock, E. H. showed up with Pauline to see how things were going, and Carlos, who had seen Cojo, told him the water pump could not be fixed till noon. E. H. said he and Pauline were going for a walk downtown and I was welcome to come along. Carlos rowed us ashore and we walked the narrow, shaded streets lined with buildings cemented together in a solid front against the sidewalks, which were just wide enough for us to walk in single file, with E. H. in the lead taking long steps, Pauline taking short steps behind him and me in the rear taking medium steps, walking on air. I was having that exhilaration which only comes in full force during your first trip on foot in a foreign city, when everything you have seen before is forgotten, everything you see and hear then being so strange you feel it is the same thing as living again, as if you had died and come to life in a different world.

"I don't care if I ever see the United States again," I announced recklessly.

"Do you really like Havana?" Pauline asked.

"It's great! I'm having the time of my life."

"I'm so glad you are. Some people are disappointed. They don't seem able to appreciate it."

The Cubans stepped off the sidewalk to let us pass and stopped and stared at us as we went by. We passed many policemen and soldiers with rifles and they nodded their heads at us because we were Americans and they knew Americans never throw bombs or start revolutions but think only of having a good time spending American dollars. We came out of the cool narrow streets into the open, hot sun of the Prado and turned up the Prado on the marble walk in the center, under cover of shade trees, between the wide traffic lanes on both sides. An American beggar got up from one of the concrete benches along the walk and asked E. H. for a dime. I saw E. H. reach in his pocket for a large coin, which the fellow accepted ungratefully—as if he had more coming—and we went on to a café across the Prado from the Capitolio where they served beer on the sidewalk in the shade. While we sat there, resting after the walk and drinking the Hatuey Cerveza, a street photographer wanted to take our picture and E. H. let him do it. It was a very marvelous life, I thought, when you can make a business of living for the pleasure there is to be got out of it, and I was having a fine time.

E. H. hired a taxi to take us back, and when we stopped at the Ambos Mundos Hotel, a block from the waterfront, the driver demanded twice the usual fare, which E. H. paid in disgust, knowing he was overcharged because we were Americans.

10

A Marlin for Mummy

BY NOON, the rebuilt water pump was back in, and we were all set to fish. E. H. started up the engines and steered out toward the stream, while I stood at the stern to see how the pumps were pumping and reported every big squirt I saw come out.

It was a clear day, hot in the sun and cool in the shade on the water and the Gulf Stream was running smooth with a strong current in close, as we could see by the trail of garbage in the slick between the current of the stream and the countercurrent along the shore, the garbage coming from the barge that was towed out of Havana and tipped in the stream every morning. Before he came to the slick, E. H. turned off the motor to let the boat coast across, to avoid catching the floating rags and weeds in the propeller. Carlos took a fresh two-pound cero mackerel from under the chopped ice and pushed a hook down its mouth, out the side and back through, leaving only the point protruding, and tied its mouth shut tight on the shank of the hook and other cords around the head and body, spat on it for good luck and dropped it over the side. It trolled smooth and lifelike through the water without turning. He fixed two more baits, one for a second rod and one as a spare, and E. H. turned the wheel over to him.

"Yi! Yi! A marlin! He's after you, Mummy! He'll take it!" E. H. shouted. His remarkable eyes had seen the marlin's pectoral fins extended from its sides before we had even seen the shadow, and that was how he knew it would strike. Sure enough, it came to the surface and tapped first with its bill like a sailfish. Pauline did everything right. She slacked, screwed the drag and struck into something alive that bent her rod and ran the vibrating line off her spool in long jerks. Then, fifty yards astern, we saw a small striped marlin, wet sides flashing silver in the high sun, jump clear out of the water, sword up, turn a somersault high in the air and go down sword-first without a splash. It repeated the jump, somersault and dive in the same place six times in succession and every time we saw the marlin jump we heard another "Yi!" from E. H. at the wheel. The marlin sounded to make his run and Pauline calmly detained him, persuaded him to turn and began leading him toward the boat, slowly, being handicapped by a rod with a handle that was too long for her.

"I can't get any leverage," she explained.

"You're doing fine, Mummy."

"But it's so slow with this rod. I can hardly reach."

"We'll fix you up another one. You've got him convinced now."

She brought the fish to gaff in seven minutes. It was a striped marlin weighing sixty-four pounds, not much bigger than a good-sized sailfish, but it was a marlin and having it on board made everybody happy.

"Isn't that a fine start for the first day, Mummy?"

"I'm delighted."

"We've been out only about fifteen minutes and we've got a marlin on board already. You fought him very well, Mummy."

"I'm sure I did."

"Carlos will fix you up another rod. Did you notice how he jumped? That fish was an athlete."

"I wish I'd had the camera ready," I said.

"We'll get a picture of him when we go in tonight."

"I wish I could have got the jumps."

"There'll be others."

Carlos said he believed that catching a marlin right off the bat like that the first day out was a sign of good luck for the whole summer. However, we saw no more fish that afternoon and we came in before sunset to take a picture of Pauline with her marlin, the first marlin for the *Pilar*.

"If we'd had a daughter we planned to name her Pilar," Pauline told me. "That explains the name of our boat."

Juan cooked supper on board, and when it was ready we sat on the bunks around the table in the cabin, E. H. pouring the imported Castilian wine into glasses filled with chopped ice and Juan bringing in the food. Juan stood by the table, straight and proud, talking to E. H. in such a loud, unrestrained voice I was surprised the way E. H. listened, unoffended, and sometimes replied in the same loud tones.

"There's something I don't like about Juan," Pauline said.

"The only trouble with Juan is he hasn't learned how to behave," E. H. replied. "He's a good cook."

"He's much too forward."

"You can't expect him to know anything, Mummy. He's always cooked on fishing smacks and he's never learned when not to talk. He thinks he's obliged to be sociable."

"I don't like the way he acts."

"We'll tone him down after a while, Mummy, but I don't want to hurt his feelings."

"I wish we didn't have him."

"I don't know where I could find a better man. He has a talent for cooking and he's fast. You saw how he tried to help today, when Carlos was gaffing the fish. He'll soon learn how to handle the wheel, and he's just the sort of a man I need. You won't be on board more than a few days all season, chances are, Mummy, but of course if you can't stand to have Juan around I'll let him go."

"Anyway, if we sleep on board tonight, I'd rather he'd not be around."

"Sure. I'll tell him he can have the night off as soon as he's through."

Juan was glad to have the night ashore, which he accepted as a special favor, and, leaving the dishes in the sink for me to wash, he got into the skiff with Carlos and I rowed them ashore, bringing the boat back.

That night there were three of us on board. I slept on the bunk up front, Ernest and Pauline in the cabin.

11

The Man Who Wanted to Marry Ginger Rogers

E. H. AND PAULINE were sitting on the afterdeck in the dark, enjoying the cool night air over the water with that cozy feeling of isolation you get when you lay at anchor in a dark harbor, where the people on shore cannot come near you or see you, yet you see them walking under the street lamps and drinking beer at the bar of the corner café. We saw a small man in a white suit come out to the dock with a woman, and the man called in a weak voice, "Hemingway! Hemingway!"

"*¡Qué tal,* Gattorno!" E. H. answered. Antonio Gattorno, the Cuban artist, and his beautiful wife came on board with a burst of happy explanations in French and Spanish that was musical and delightful to listen to, and during the entire evening they continued as merry as children around a Christmas tree. It was amazing how many people E. H. made happy when they were near him. E. H. asked me to mix some drinks, not forgetting myself, and while we sipped the cocktails, Lillian Gattorno smoked Hemingway's American cigarettes in a sort of ecstasy, because Lucky Strikes were the popular brand the Hollywood actresses smoked in the advertisements.

I slept on the afterdeck. When I heard Carlos calling my new name, "Arnoldo!," from the dock, it was Sunday morning. I rowed after him in the *Bumby,* helped him load the block of ice, beer and baits and tried to understand him when he said he had stood on the dock half an hour shouting my name before I awoke, but it was no use, I couldn't savvy Spanish. The traffic in the harbor was already lively. Many launches were taking the soldiers who had spent Saturday night ashore back to their bunks in the fortress. Others were filled with old and young people dressed for pleasure trips. Even the fishing smacks lying at Casa Blanca had their sails raised high and white in the bright morning sun, dressed up because it was Sunday. E. H. and Pauline went to church and I had a walk ashore. There were not very many automobiles on the streets, few pedestrians, no loafers around the dock or café; the shops were padlocked, and the quiet, deserted streets gave me that Forlorn Sunday Morning feeling, so I didn't enjoy my stroll very much.

It was different when I returned to the ship. E. H. was on board with his guests, ready to go, and there was the usual brisk action—starting the motors, hauling the anchor and getting the rods out. The sordid influence of Sunday exists only on land, where the usual activity is stopped, imposing funereal silence where there is naturally noise and movement. It never followed us out of the harbor, for one day is like any other day on the water except for changes in the weather and the run of fish. That morning there were three guests: Gattorno and his wife and Lopez Mendez, another artist.

Lopez Mendez had brought along a portable phonograph, which we set up on the shelf by the wheel. Going out of the harbor, they started up a rousing Spanish song, singing it with the abandonment of drunkards feeling marvelous, none of them having had a drink yet, E. H. joining in with a lusty bass. It was the first time I'd heard him sing and that first day was the happiest fishing day of the year.

Gattorno was a truly great artist and he had the look of one. He had a beautiful face, clear, steady blue eyes, black hair and a very frail body with slightly stooped and rounded shoulders. E. H. said he had studied several years in Paris and now depended entirely on his art for his living and had a hard time of it. Lopez Mendez was a good artist, not a great one, yet he made more money because he commercialized his art in a department store. Lopez, distinguished looking, did not laugh so much or show his emotions on his face as Gattorno did. When Gattorno was happy, he felt like singing and beating time on the fish box with his fists, and there was no stopping him. E. H. said he was the youngest man he knew. He had a spontaneity that rarely survives childhood and his happiness was infectious and made everybody join in when he sang. These were the first artists I had ever seen and I was curious about them.

Carlos steered the *Pilar* straight out to the purple Gulf water and turned her to the right with the current, following it into the morning sun on a parallel course with the land, a mile from shore, with E. H. and Pauline fishing the marlin baits in the cool shade of the cockpit roof, Lopez Mendez sitting between them holding a rod with a feather for wahoo and the Gattornos sitting on the fish box facing them, talking, singing and laughing. Juan was below attending to his food in the galley; sometimes he came up and stood in the doorway, smoking his penny cigar and grinning at the party, but never paying any attention to Carlos, probably because Carlos was a Cubano. Carlos was very sensitive, and it must have hurt; he had been captain of a ninety-foot fishing smack in his day, and Juan had never been more than a cook and a Spaniard.

Pauline's arm grew tired from holding the heavy rod and reel and dragging the two-pound bait through the water. Lopez Mendez took her rod and I took his, the small one with the feather.

"Talk to him," Pauline said to me. "He speaks English."

"Do you speak English?" I asked Lopez, taking the chair between him and E. H.

"No. Very little. Very poor. Not much."

I was not used to the way Spanish people speak English, and could scarcely understand those simple words.

"You speak it very well," I said.

"No, not well. But I like to learn. Have you been in Hollywood?"

"Yes."

"Have you seen Ginger Rogers?"

"Only in the movies."

"I want to marry Ginger Rogers. I like her very well."

"Do you know her?"

"No. Only in the movies. But I want to marry her. I think she would make me a good wife. That is why I would like to go to Hollywood."

Lopez was half serious, half jesting, and there was a twinkle in his eye when he said it.

"Aren't there plenty women in Havana?"

"Plenty, yes." He was entirely serious now. "But I like the American girls much better. They, what do you call it? stick by a man. Love means something to them. The Spanish women are different; love, marriage, home, that means nothing to them. They love you today, and tomorrow they love somebody else. You never know where you are at. You have a home and you think you have a wife and love and happiness and you wake up some morning and you find she has gone with somebody else. You can't trust them. It is in their blood. I would like very much to marry an American girl."

"That should be easy."

"I want to marry Ginger Rogers." His eyes were twinkling again.

"She might be harder to get at."

"I know. Hollywood is more far away than Miami."

"Why don't you write her a letter?"

"It is too difficult to send your sex appeal in a letter. Some day I will go to Hollywood myself and marry Ginger Rogers."

"She might be married by then."

"That does not matter. She can get a divorce."

Ernest told me to learn a lesson from Lopez Mendez, that he was a man who really knew tragedy. At sixteen he was arrested and imprisoned as a student revolutionary in Venezuela; he was permitted to escape with his life by leaving the country only because of his youth. Dictator Gomez had seized his father's lands, and thrown him in the dungeon, and Lopez had never been able to learn if his father was still alive during the last twenty years. It was horrible to realize he might still be alive and suffering underground, and Lopez would rather think of him as dead if it were not for the hope that some day a new revolution might overthrow the government and set free the political prisoners and he might see his father again, but that chance was so slim it only made things worse. There was nothing he could do. His letters to the Venezuela government inquiring after his father's health were never answered.

In Havana, Lopez became a painter and acquired a beautiful home and a wife he loved and a daughter he loved and a friend he was very fond of. Antonio, his friend, was unlucky in money matters, so Lopez supplied him with funds and made him as welcome as a brother in his house. He knew people in the government offices, and through them he succeeded in getting Antonio an appointment to a diplomatic job in Mexico City to start him on a new career. Antonio said he was very grateful but he could not see his way clear to accept this position, having no money to buy the clothes necessary to the dignity of such an office or the steamship ticket to Mexico. Lopez loaned him four hundred dollars and Antonio departed with his host's money and then ran off with his wife and daughter, taking them with him to Mexico City and completely breaking up the home and tearing to pieces the life of Lopez Mendez. All this had happened less than a month ago, it was still raw in his mind; now, as Lopez sat fishing the other marlin bait, he preferred to joke about marrying Ginger Rogers rather than think of his personal affairs.

"You can't judge American girls by the movies," I said.

"I like American girls," he replied. "I know many. Norma Shearer is a personal friend of mine. She calls me up every time she comes to Havana. I'm her favorite escort in Havana."

"Then why don't you marry Norma Shearer?"

"A shark's after you, Lopez," E. H. interrupted. "Reel in, Arnold."

A big shark, yellow and ugly-looking in the water, uglier than anything else in the sea, giving you the same feeling you have when you see a snake on land, was following behind the mackerel bait on the surface with his fin out. I reeled in the feather, put the rod away and hauled in the teasers and the shark kept following at the same distance on the surface, four feet behind the bait.

"What shall I do?" Lopez asked.

"Nothing. Let him have it," E. H. said quietly, never excited by a shark.

"What when he takes the bait?"

"That's when you take him."

"Why does he not take it now?"

"He's a coward. He hasn't got the guts to strike right away. He's thinking it over."

"Maybe he is not hungry."

"Sharks are always hungry."

The two-hundred-pound shark followed the two-pound cero mackerel for several minutes, and then his tail swung out with a splash and Lopez had a shark on his hook instead of a dead cero mackerel. Carlos cut down the motor and let the boat move ahead slowly, just enough to keep the shark astern, and the shark went down, hauling off the line in long, heavy pulls, and Lopez Mendez, who was slim, not very strong and had never fished big fish, saw the line going into the water without being able to do anything about it.

"What shall I do?" he asked.

"Bring him in."

"But he's going the other way."

"Stop him."

"But how do you do it?"

The slow-moving shark was a good fish to learn on. E. H. had plenty of time to screw down the drag tight enough to stop the shark's run and show Lopez how to pump the rod and to reel in the slack when he lowered. It is still a hard thing to teach to a man who is working on his first big fish, or, rather, having his first big fish work on him, because his mind is excited and confused and not receptive to instruction. The first time you handle a rod and reel it seems such a clumsy apparatus, especially when a fish is running off with the line. You feel absolutely helpless, you forget to pump and you try to do the heavy work with the reel, which is impossible. It seems such an impossible job and there are so many things to think of that the advice you get confuses you all the more; you can't apply any of it and it only makes you more desperately aware of your helplessness. Lopez struggled and lost line, tried to get it back and lost more, wearing himself out and doing nothing with the shark until his arms weakened and he had to give up and turn the rod over to Ernest. E. H. reeled in the shark as easily as he would a smashed bait, leading it to the stern on the surface. Carlos, standing on the fish box as agile as a cat, sank the gaff into the water. E. H. stood by, holding the rod with the drag off and line clear in case the shark got away and had to be led in again.

"Bring me the pistol," he said.

I got the automatic out of its holster in the rubber bag, handed it to E. H. and held his rod while he shot his initials into the top of the shark's head. The shark was still swinging his tail and snapping his jaws, showing his big mouth full of sharp, white teeth, when Juan and Carlos, pulling together on the gaff handle, raised him halfway out of the water at the stern until his flat head was above the fish box and Carlos could get at him and club him over the nose the way market fishermen kill sharks, stunning him and stopping his tail and giving him a few more to make sure before they pulled him on board to take the hook out. It was a common shark, known as the galano in Cuba. It had swallowed the bait, and the hook was so far down its throat Carlos had to cut it out of his side. That made a mess, and after we heaved the shark overboard and watched him sink Carlos was kept busy dipping buckets of water and washing the blood off the deck.

Gattorno was looking sad. He was shocked by the slaughter and the sight of blood, and he felt sorry for the shark. I think he even protested to E. H. in the shark's defense, although I could not be sure, being unable to understand the language. Anyway, he looked very sad, and it took him a long time to get over it. To E. H., killing a shark was not a pretty spectacle, but it was satisfying, like killing a snake on land that would kill you if it had a chance. Lopez was feeling better all the time; he was forgetting the part E. H. played in landing the shark and making himself believe that he, Lopez, had caught it.

After cleaning up the shark mess, we refreshed ourselves with ice-cold bottles of Hatuey beer and continued trolling with the current down the Cuban coast. It became my job to turn the records on Lopez's portable phonograph. Whenever they wanted music, E. H. would say to me, *"Maestro! Mùsica!"* By noon we were several miles down the green coast and the top of the Morro Castle tower was all we could see of Havana. We had passed the small fisherman's town of Cojímar and were opposite the cove of Bacuranao when E. H. told Carlos to turn in to shore.

"That's the cove where they landed the Chinks," E. H. told me, referring to "One Trip Across."

It seemed a long time since I had read that story. I was living in Minneapolis then, trying to become a writer by writing from the time I got up in the morning until I was completely exhausted at night, and after my stories cooled off they stank. In my fits of depression I read books, and most of them were unsatisfactory. I read magazines, hoping to learn something from the modern writers, and they were worse. Then, coming across that story by Ernest Hemingway, there was as much difference between it and the others as there is between night and day. I was fed up with elegant phrases and forced plots and here at last I found a story told in the words of a tough fisherman that was the most convincing thing I had ever read. I did not know what it was that made the story good, but that was the way I wanted to write!—not knowing there were thousands of others who wanted the same thing. I knew the writer was alive and I hoped he would give me a hint on how to set to work in writing a story. If I could understand something of the art that lay beneath it, learning it from him, I thought I still might have a chance. That was three months ago. Now I was on board his yacht, fishing with him, and we were heading toward the cove where the fisherman in his story had squeezed the Chink's throat till it cracked.

"You must know this coast pretty well," I said.

"You've got to before you can write about it," E. H. replied. "When you start to write a story you have your setting and your people. You know them absolutely and you know what they would do. You start off with an interesting situation and invent the action. The story writes itself."

"And you don't have any idea of the plot to start with?"

"No. All you have is your setting and characters."

"Then, if you don't have any plot, how do you know you can write a story?"

"You know that. When you've got the stuff you know you've got a story. But the sea is the hardest place there is to get a story. You can be out here ten years and nothing ever happens. A war on land is different. You can be on a battlefield three months and you've got a novel."

We reeled in the baits, and E. H. steered the *Pilar* into the cove past the rocky point on the left where the water was deepest and Carlos threw out the anchor. The cove was muddy from a small river running into it and on the land side a fisherman's boat was beached on the sand. His shack was in the green brush near the old lookout tower, where in the old days guards watched for the pirate ships and signaled to Havana with smoke fires when they saw them coming. Now this fishing shack was used as a lookout station to signal contraband boats at sea, letting them know by hanging out clothes on the clothesline when the *Rurales,* soldiers on horseback, were in the area. E. H. said he might want to use it in a story sometime.

We got into our bathing trunks, dove off the stern and swam toward the beach. I swam as fast as I was able, afraid there might be sharks or barracuda in the dark water and expecting a shark to come on me any minute and cut my legs off. I never worried about sharks in front biting off my head. In the water the expected danger was always from the rear. I felt better when we were walking on the beach toward the square fortress built of rock. The fisherman loaned us a ladder to climb up on the inside through a small square hole in the middle of the ceiling, which used to give the guards the advantage of being able to pull the ladder up after them and make themselves safe from attack. From the top of the tower we saw the Gulf Stream, as the Cuban guards did four hundred years ago; we saw an oil tanker and several fishing boats, but no pirate ships. We returned to the beach and loafed on the sand until Juan raised the white towel on the mast to let us know dinner was ready and we swam back to the boat.

Juan made a reputation for himself with that meal. He served five dishes of Pauline's marlin meat prepared in five different ways, each a masterpiece, and the eaters scattered around the cockpit with plates in their laps talking about the wonderful food and Juan's talent as a cook. Juan stood in the doorway, too happy to talk, watching us with a broad grin on his face. He was an artist in his line and he took an artist's satisfaction in seeing the public appreciate his work. E. H. told Juan the food was very good and decided not to tell him until later, when it would not offend him, that even if we had more marlin meat than we could use, he need not consider it an extravagance to buy other kinds of food to go with it.

"Carlos is jealous because Juan has made such a hit," E. H. told Pauline. "We'd better not brag him up too much."

We never did see Juan eat or wash dishes. He was too democratically brought up to think it improper for the cook to eat with the shipowner and his guests, so his reasons for eating his food out of sight in the galley must have been more complicated. He was probably too much of an artist to let his public see what he thought of his own work. Juan stayed on the afterdeck enjoying the contented looks on the faces of the eaters and watched Carlos, who considered himself the captain, wash the dishes and pots in a pail of salt water dipped from the sea.

We lay in the cove another hour after dinner, resting and talking and laughing at Lopez Mendez show off his English by reading the society news in the Miami *Herald.* He read with such feeling it made marvelous entertainment, but Gattorno couldn't understand English and was looking sad, probably still feeling sorry for the shark, so the conversation turned to Spanish, leaving me out and Gattorno in, and E. H. told them about how his friend Sidney Franklin, the American bullfighter, suffered from the *cornada* he received in his last bullfight. The bull had passed, and Sidney was making a low bow to the crowd, and the bull turned and charged from the rear, driving his horn through Sidney's rectum and up into his intestines. That made Gattorno forget the shark and he began to feel better.

When we started back toward Havana in the afternoon we were again headed into the sun, fishing in the shade where it is always cool on the Gulf Stream, even off Cuba in the summertime. There are not many small fish on that side of the stream, and there was no action while we sat watching the baits trailing behind through the purple water and waiting for something big. "Something very big" would be a 1,500-pound marlin. Hemingway had seen a marlin in the market caught with a handline by market fishermen that weighed 1,250 pounds dressed, with its head and tail off and the insides taken out, leaving 1,250 pounds of solid meat ready to be cut up into steaks. Someday if he was lucky, he might run into a fish like that and land it and break every record of rod and reel set by marlin fishermen and leave them something to shoot at. That was something to live for. It might be a man's luck to fish the stream all his life and never see such a fish, but there was also the chance that it would come any minute, while we listened to Gattorno and Lopez singing. That was why E. H. would never take a drink while we were fishing; he might have to wait for years, but he wanted to be ready, in perfect shape, when the big fish came. Fishing dolphin and sailfish off Key West had been a diversion to rest the mind; this was serious business, the seriousness of which only E. H. and Carlos could understand. They were the only two real fishermen on board, the rest of us were a party on a pleasure cruise up and down the coast. Gattorno, refreshed with a gin drink, was sitting on the fish box feeling marvelous again, singing as loud as he could with his weak lungs, and keeping time tapping his empty glass against the mahogany till it cracked. When he was happy he had to sing, and singing made him even happier until his throat went dry. When Gattorno stopped, his wife began. She had copies of popular American songs and sang them without much feeling, having difficulty in reading them off in a foreign language.

"Why don't you sing some of the old Spanish songs?" I asked her. "They're much prettier."

E. H. turned his head. He always overheard everything that was said on board, although he usually gave no sign of it, and my remark had interested him. He probably thought it was conceit.

"Oh, I like so much the American songs," Mrs. Gattorno said.

"Why?"

"I like everything in the United States very much. I like the American cigarettes and the American language and the American movies. I like it all very much. Sometime I like to go there to the United States."

She drew a deep sigh of yearning and gave me the impression that life is very sad to a young woman who wants to go to the States and can't.

"Where in the United States would you like to go?"

"HOLLYWOOD!"

"Hollywood isn't very pretty. Havana is much prettier."

Lillian Gattorno had never thought that there might be a difficulty in getting into the movies. She thought the railway fare to Hollywood was all that stood in the way of her becoming a star, and once she got there it would be easy. She would let Clark Gable and other men in the business make love to her while the photographers stood around with their cameras and then she would go and see herself in the theaters. It would be a wonderful life.

She had reason for being so sure of herself because she was very beautiful to look at in the flesh, and her husband, who was a great artist and ought to know, must have told her so many times. Apart from her lovely figure, she had a sleek tanned skin, clear blue eyes and glossy brown hair, all very pleasant features in a woman who is sitting beside you, but none of them worth much on a photograph. Her face was too narrow for the movies, her eyes too close together and she did not know how to act.

"All the women in the States would like to be movie stars, too," I told her, "but competition is pretty tough. Not many make it."

I could see her mind was sealed and my argument had no effect.

"Sometime, someday, maybe I will go to Hollywood," she answered dreamily.

12

Dinner with Lopez

THE AFTERNOON offshore wind scattered rainclouds over the sky, giving the sun material to work with in making a beautiful display of colors when it set in the sea. We were nearing the Morro Castle, not having seen a marlin all day, having reeled in the baits and left the feather out for tarpon in the harbor, so I served the drinks and sat down beside Lopez Mendez, who was watching the sun dip into the water and sink.

"I invite you to dine with me tonight," he said.

"Thanks, but maybe I'll have to stay on the ship."

"I talked to Ernest. He says it's all right if you come back at nine o'clock."

"Thanks, but I haven't got any clothes."

"You don't need clothes. What you wear now is good enough."

"Many thanks. Then I'll come."

"Some other night I'll take you on a real Cuban party. How do you like these Cuban girls?"

"They're all right."

"No! You must not say just 'all right.' You must say 'Wonderful! Marvelous! Beautiful!' I know one girl you would like. Her name is Margarita. She is crazy for Americans."

I didn't answer him.

E. H. told me to go, and I went with Lopez to the building downtown where he had taken an apartment after having closed his house when his wife ran off. He had two rooms with tile floors and in the biggest one a small portrait he had painted of his mother hung on the wall. There was a radio by the low wooden bed and a cupboard where he kept his whiskey. A dark-complexioned young man came out of the other bedroom, and Lopez introduced him as his cousin, Enrique, another expatriated revolutionary.

"Enrique is an aviator," Lopez said. "He has been in the States. Therefore he speaks English much better than me, but he has a bad Chicago accent."

Lopez poured whiskey into three glasses and mumbled a few words in Spanish while he filled them with ice and soda.

"Be a gentleman," Enrique told Lopez. "Speak English when we have a guest who does not understand Spanish."

"It is easier for you to be a gentleman. Go ahead. Help yourself," Lopez said. "This one for you, Maestro. Drink. Bottoms up. Is that what the Americans say?"

"It's their favorite expression."

"Very well. Bottoms up. Go ahead and drink. Do not be afraid to get drunk."

Lopez still felt the effects of a hangover from a Saturday night party. Two drinks of whiskey straightened him up, and he went into the bathroom to shave and came out wearing an immaculate cream-colored suit, looking much better and feeling like a gentleman, which he was, and acting with a more sprightly ease and dignity that matched his change of clothes. He took us downstairs and across the street to a corner drugstore, and we sat up to the counter on the swivel stools. Lopez ordered wine and a tray of oysters with limes.

"I have been so disappointed in love, marriage, friendship, everything," Lopez said, squeezing lime juice on the oysters. "For a while

I was thinking I should kill myself. Then I thought, if I kill myself that will do me no good. I must forget and make new friends and start over again. Last night I get very drunk. I never used to drink too much or run after women. I only am trying to forget. A man cannot forget alone. I saw you on the boat today and I said to myself, that is one boy I like to know. I talked to Ernest about you. He tells me you are a writer. You have the soul of an artist."

"I'd like to be a writer, but I don't suppose I'll ever make it."

"I write, too; little, short humorous pieces, sometimes. But I am like the dust. I am like the wind."

"That's my trouble, too."

"Whatever you do, never be an intellectual. Be a man! Always remember that. That's what I like about Ernest and that's what he likes about me. Always remember that. Never be an intellectual. That's the worst thing that could happen to you. Be a man!"

A woman came in and sat down on the other side of Lopez. He introduced her as Maruca, one of his new friends who was helping him forget. The three of us went to a Spanish restaurant where the plates were as thick and heavy as stove lids and big chunks of Cuban bread and bottles of Hatuey beer were served with the food. The woman could not understand English and had nothing to say in Spanish and Lopez and I kept the conversation going while he poured the beer, me saying, "Thanks, I have plenty," and he replying, "Never say plenty. Drink! There is always more." The meal ended with a small cup of black coffee and a cigar. Lopez ushered me into a taxi and when we arrived at the dock we heard a bell somewhere tolling the hour. It was exactly nine o'clock.

13

The Porpoises

E. H. AND PAULINE came on board alone Monday morning, and it seemed unusually quiet and peaceful as we headed toward the stream. There were no guests, no singing or loud laughter and no talking, we knowing what to do, understanding one another, and E. H. under no obligation to entertain anybody. None of the Cubans ever had time to come on board the *Pilar* during a work day. For them, going out in a boat was something you did on Sunday. So they were busy with their routine lives, and we were like a family that stays in the house and relaxes after the party is over and the guests are gone. Even the phonograph stayed out of sight far below.

It was not a good day to fish, being cloudy and dark and still with a weak current and a flat sea. What E. H. wanted was a bright sun, so the marlin could see the baits at a distance, and a northeast wind to kick up a choppy sea against a strong current. He said a rough sea would bring them to the top because they liked the movement of the waves, but now, when it was calm, if there were any marlin they were traveling deep down, and unless a good breeze came up in the afternoon chances were we would not see one and it would be just luck if we did.

Half a mile out in the stream we threw out the teasers and let out the baits, Ernest with one rod, me with the other, on a day when all the signs were wrong for action. Pauline had a light rod with the feather. We were having a quiet, uneventful boat ride on a dull day when Carlos, at the wheel, shouted in great excitement, "*¡Mira! Mira!* Look ahead!"

We looked ahead and saw that the sea had become black with the backs of an incredible herd of rolling porpoises traveling against the current. From the boat to shore, a mile away, the water was covered with them and they were rolling as far as we could see on the other side toward the stream. The school was at least two miles wide and there seemed to be no end to the run ahead. There were thousands of porpoises everywhere in sight, and those we saw at any one time coming up for air and rolling with a slow, wheel-like motion were only a few of the number near the surface. They were passing under the boat four layers deep, everywhere side by side as thick as a herd of stampeding cattle, and we were in the middle of that great stampede, moving against it, wedging through and over them untouched.

"Reel in," E. H. said. "Get your Kodak. They might start jumping."

They were becoming livelier, several shooting out over the water in slow, easy, arc-like jumps and one coming up three feet over a swell. Several started jumping alongside the boat as if to look us over and see if they might recognize any of us.

"Wow! Did you see that?" I asked.

"Don't waste your shots. There's plenty of time."

"There's another one. Look at him jump!"

"Don't take any pictures unless you get them up close."

They were jumping higher and higher, their big round bodies and flat horizontal tails making long graceful curves over the water. When you see one porpoise jump it is a beautiful sight, although not very exciting, but when you see a dozen of them in the air and the backs of thousands of others rolling, it is a spectacle—and that spectacle made me yell. I danced on the deck in a delirious ecstasy, yelling in a high-pitched voice whenever I saw a porpoise and seeing them all the time.

"Yi! Yi! Yi! Three of them at a time! Lookit! Oh, boy! Oh boy! Wow! Eeeeyi! Yi!"

I heard E. H. say quietly, "Look, Mummy," and she answered, "Aren't they wonderful?" E. H. was a fisherman, and I thought he had a greater emotional reaction in seeing a marlin jump because there was a struggle in it between a man and a fish and there was no fighting in this exhibition of porpoises playing. To me it was not the struggle that produced the emotion, it was the spectacle of the fish jumping, and I got exactly the same kick whether the fish was free or had a hook in its mouth. I didn't see how the sight of a single swordfish could compare with thousands of porpoises, the fullgrown ones bigger than the biggest marlin ever caught, a dozen of them jumping at once all around us, not stopping at five or six jumps, but jumping continuously wherever we cared to look.

A black porpoise ten feet long shot up alongside the boat so close we could have reached him with the gaff and so high at the top of his curve he was even with our heads as we stood on the cockpit deck watching him sail slowly through the air in a long, easy jump that could have cleared the cabin roof.

"Did you get that one?" E. H. asked.

"I got him! I got him! I got him! Oh, boy! I got him!" I answered.

"Good," E. H. said.

"Oh, boy! I got him right at the top. I got him just before he started coming down!"

"Good," E. H. said.

The jumping had just begun. As if the big porpoise had set an example, others began to imitate and improve on it, taking long horizontal jumps ten feet above the water. Carlos was almost crying he was so excited, and Juan's lean face was cut in half with his wide grin, looking as happy as if he had cooked for a presidential banquet. E. H. and Pauline went up in the bow, E. H. taking pictures with the movie camera, and I sat behind them shouting hysterically and taking snapshots with my Kodak, having, truly, the happiest time of my life. Here there was no need for emotional restraint, as there was when we were fighting a fish. There was nothing that had to be done or thought about and we were free to watch the spectacle of flying porpoises and enjoy it. An aeronautic competition had begun, and it seemed the porpoises were trying to decide which could jump the highest. We saw one porpoise jump straight up to an unbelievable height and turn and dive into the same boil where he had come up. He must have cleared the water by thirty or forty feet. It was such an amazing performance I could have not been more astonished if he had jumped into the sky out of sight and never come down. I had my Kodak pointed at him but forgot about taking a picture until after he had disappeared. Then, a quarter of a mile away, toward shore, we saw six come out together and climb side by side straight up toward the sky. At the top of their jump they appeared to be suspended motionless in midair, heads erect, hanging from an invisible line, before they turned and went down. Then hundreds of them began taking long, horizontal leaps and the air was filled with them, in the distance looking like a flock of birds flying low over the water, swooping down, coming up and diving again.

Suddenly the jumping stopped, and the thousands of porpoises were rolling leisurely on the surface as they had in the beginning. We followed them several miles, hoping they might start jumping again, but the performance was over and we were wondering whether we could believe what we had just seen.

E. H. counted forty-eight porpoises playing in front of the bow, and when we turned downstream they turned with us and went ahead for about a mile and then turned and went back to the main school. We put away the cameras, let out the baits and continued trolling for marlin toward the cove.

Now that it was over, I felt self-conscious about all my excitement. What I had seen really shook me up. I wondered why Ernest had shown no reaction.

"Did you ever see anything like that before?" I asked him.

"No," he answered.

"Has Carlos?"

"No."

"Lord! That was some sight, wasn't it? I'm not over it yet."

"Don't ever try to write about it. It's impossible to describe. No writer that has ever lived could give the reader the emotion."

Then I knew E. H. had felt it as much as I had, the difference being that he had his emotions under control.

"How high did those six jump, do you think?"

"About thirty feet. They're ten feet long and they can jump three times their length straight up."

"How many would you say there were?"

"Maybe ten thousand. They were spread out two miles wide and at least six miles long, and you saw how thick they were."

"Do you think we'll ever see anything like that again?"

"No, and it may be nobody ever will. Let's get the log before I forget it."

E. H. did not forget it. Some years later the porpoises of that day appeared in the dream of the fisherman in *The Old Man and the Sea*. "He did not dream of lions but instead of a vast school of porpoises that stretched for eight or ten miles and it was the time of their mating and they would leap high into the air and return into the same hole they made in the water when they leaped."

14

To See It As It Is ...

THE NEXT DAY we were out again. Fishing had become our business and our way of life. We were out there to fish every day of the marlin season. E. H., sitting in his fishing chair and watching the bait, dictated a description of what we had seen and I wrote it down.

"This log is fun for me," I said when we were through. "I think I'm learning something."

"It's good practice. You see the same things I do. Seeing a thing and writing it are two entirely different things. Anybody can see a thing, but to see it as it really is and be able to write it as it happened, that's what makes a writer. You'll see how I put it down and you'll learn what to watch for. You'll learn how to be accurate and you'll learn something about handling your sentences. It's good for me, too. It gives me practice in dictating."

"If those pictures turn out, do you suppose I might use them with a piece for a sports magazine?"

"Certainly."

"I've got the piece about Key West rewritten. Where do you go to get stamps in Havana?"

"I'll ask Pauline to take it with her to Key West. She can mail it from there."

"Swell."

"Don't get discouraged, now, if they don't take it, because that doesn't mean a thing. I had them coming back for years when I knew I was writing good stuff."

"I tried to write some last night, but I couldn't."

"Nobody can write after he's been on the water all day."

"Then maybe I won't be able to write anything all the time we're over here."

"Don't let that worry you. You might get a chance if we lay up a day. I want to write, too, that's what I live for, but I can't while we're fishing. You won't be losing any time. You'll be getting material that will be invaluable to you later on if you keep to writing as a career, and you'll be meeting interesting people that you might never have been able to meet otherwise. The people you meet here are a lot different from those you meet in the States. Here, when a man's your friend, it means something."

"Do you use these people in your fiction?"

"Some of them."

"What's the best experience a man can have for writing fiction?"

"A war. Wars have made many great writers. Or an unhappy childhood. A disappointment in love. Almost anything that is bad for other people is good for a writer. And, at forty, when other men start slipping, a writer's mind clears. How about some music, Maestro?"

"Which one?"

"Jimmy Durante."

" 'Hot Patatta'?"

"That's it."

Carlos headed the boat into the cove. We swam, had crawfish salad, avocados and sliced pineapple with Castilian wine and lay at anchor an hour or more after the meal, resting on the bunks and reading in the cool shade. There was always plenty to read. E. H. brought the Havana and New York papers every day and the magazines *Time, New Yorker* and *Esquire* when they came out, and there were four shelves of books in the lockers. Then, in the afternoon, we trolled back into Havana harbor without seeing any fish, with the same baits Carlos had put on in the morning.

The next day we had the same luck, trolling the same baits through the empty purple water without seeing a fish. E. H. said the current seemed to be picking up and the breeze shifting to the northeast in the afternoon was a good sign if it would keep blowing and bring the marlin to the surface. There must be marlin in the stream, he said, because it was now the middle of July and that was the time for their biggest run. Carlos had fished marlin off Havana ever since he was a boy, and his father and grandfather had fished them before him; every summer they could remember, the marlin had made their run against the current close to the Cuban shore. Nobody knew where they came from or where they went to, but every year they came back. Usually, the run began in late May. This year it had been delayed over a month; if they were ever coming, they were due in late July, and we might expect to find the stream full of fish any day.

"How many is the most you've seen at a time?" I asked E. H.

"About sixty."

"Do you think we might ever see as many marlin as we did porpoises?"

"Anything is possible in the stream."

"When will they have the porpoise pictures ready?"

"Maybe tonight."

Every evening at sundown, when we came in to anchor, a few of Hemingway's friends would be waiting for us at the dock. I would bring them on board in the *Bumby* and they would sit on the bunks and fishing chairs in the afterdeck, talking Spanish with E. H. while I mixed drinks and refilled their glasses until they raised their arms and protested they had enough. Besides Gattorno and his wife and Lopez Mendez, there were several others who came regularly, including Julio, Cojo and Aliende. Sometimes they all came on board the same night. That was the time and place E. H. entertained his guests. When he went alone to the room in the Ambos Mundos Hotel, the party was over.

Julio was the pilot, a big man with a loud, hoarse voice and violent gestures. He met the ships coming in, steered them into the harbor—temporarily taking over the authority of the captain—and steered them out when they left. Julio had a good job and good pay, and, in partnership with a Havana physician, he owned a small sailboat lying at anchor near the *Pilar.* Carlos was very fond of Julio, having taken him fishing marlin and taught him all he knew about the sea and advised him to study for the pilot's examination when he was a boy. Carlos had made Julio what he was and was proud of him. He might, at times, be a nuisance, but he was useful to get contraband past the Customs.

Cojo, of course, was the mechanic on the government payroll who walked on his heels, having had the toes of both his feet cut off in an accident. He had repaired the water pump of our big motor and refused to take pay, saying it was nothing, he was happy to do it as a friend. He was a good-hearted, middle-aged bachelor who loved food and was getting plump because it was difficult for him to walk and he did not feel like taking any more exercise than necessary with his crippled feet. He also loved good liquor, and whenever he came on board I put plenty of whiskey in his drink, knowing he would refuse a second glass.

Aliende was Hemingway's purchasing agent, and whenever E. H. or Pauline needed anything downtown they let him buy it for them.

"Haven't you suspected what makes Aliende so thin?" E. H. asked me once.

"Isn't he just naturally that way?"

"No."

"Is it TB?"

"No. Starvation. He doesn't get enough to eat."

"But his boys look fat."

"Sure. He sees to it that they get plenty."

"And his clothes look good."

"If they didn't, he'd lose his self-respect. Clothes mean a great deal in this country."

Aliende, tall and gaunt, standing beside his two half-grown, healthy sons, used to wait for us at the dock to see whether there was anything E. H. needed downtown. He didn't want to bother them, he would explain to me in good English, there were so many already, he didn't want to go on board. He thought perhaps E. H. might be needing something. Had I heard him say? No, I hadn't; he would have to talk to E. H. about it, I would answer, and Aliende would come on board and find a seat, obviously sorry he was taking up so much room and making the boat so crowded and would listen without much interest in the conversation, no matter how lively it was, not wanting to interrupt it with his business, while he waited for E. H. to tell him if there was anything he wanted. E. H. would tell me to mix Aliende a drink, which Aliende would decline, and when I made him one anyway he would accept it half-heartedly in order not to be conspicuous. The only time you saw any sign of life in him was when Pauline talked of his two handsome sons waiting for him on the dock.

All these people were on board, making a boatful, soon after we came in that evening, when a small man came out on the dock shouting in Spanish and waving his arm.

"It's the Gallego," E. H. said. "You'd better get him. He's got your pictures."

I made good time rowing to the dock. I reached for the photographer's envelope in the Gallego's hand and took out the prints, trembling with excitement. One of the pictures caught a close broadside view of a porpoise ten feet above the water and the boil beneath him where he had come up. It was the most remarkable porpoise picture ever taken, I thought, or at least better than any of those Zane Grey had in his book, and if I could get porpoise pictures like that, why not the marlin? I visualized a big future for myself as a photographer on the Gulf Stream, E. H. catching the fish and me getting the pictures of the marlin in every conceivable position, as they jumped out of the sea, keeping them alive in action forever. I had always been fond of taking pictures, and now, with the prospect of marlin before me and one success already, I was crazy about it. One difference I didn't realize, of course, was that marlin do not come up to the boat to look it over when they jump.

Being in a hurry to show E. H. the pictures, I forgot to invite the Gallego on board and had begun pulling off the dock without him when he jumped and landed on the stern seat. He was another irregular eater who lost weight in the wintertime and fattened during the summer months when E. H. fished off Havana. He was a taxi driver when he had a taxi, but every spring when E. H. returned to Havana, the Gallego would not have a car, lacking the money for a deposit, and E. H. would start him up in business and patronize him all summer.

The Gallego stepped on board, bowing several times and saying, "Very good afternoon, ladies and gentlemen, *cómo está? ¿Cómo está? ¿Comó está?*" Then to me, "You have *vino para me?*"

"What?"

"¡Vino! ¡Vino!"

"What does he say?"

"He wants wine," E. H. said. "Give him a glass."

The Gallego followed me into the galley, where he drank a glass of wine in one gulp, had it refilled and took it out to the cockpit sipping it slowly, very happy to be among friends and to know that good days were ahead for at least three months.

"How did the pictures turn out?" E. H. asked.

"Swell. Here, aren't they marvelous?"

"One good one. How many did you take?"

"Sixteen."

"We'll get film packs for the Graflex tonight. You'll soon learn how to use it. It's very simple."

15

The Fighting Marlin

THE NEXT MORNING, E. H. came on board alone. Pauline had returned to Key West to be with the family. They had first planned on moving everyone to Cuba for the summer, but decided against it because of an outbreak of polio. It was blowing a steady northeast breeze which would increase in the afternoon, the current was picking up and E. H. said it looked like a good day for marlin. He offered to bet two to one that we would have a fish on board before night, and if I had been a betting man, I could have made some easy money because E. H. never offered a bet unless the odds were against him.

E. H. and I sat trolling in the new swivel fishing chairs he had had built and fastened to the deck after we came to Havana. They had sockets for the rods and we could now fish with one hand holding the loose spool and the other free. The new ones were comfortable and solid and there was no danger of falling out. In the old wicker chairs we had held the rods in our laps with both hands. The chairs used to slide around the deck and sometimes tip over in the rough seas. I compared the old chairs to bucking broncs, and E. H. said, "When I was in Wyoming, they asked what I did for a living and I told them I was a writer. They thought I said rider. I've never been able to ride a horse."

We sat with the rods pointing off to the sides, with our bare feet resting on the fish box and the long visors of our fishing caps shielding our eyes from the sun's glare, with olive oil on our noses, watching the baits trail smoothly behind the teasers.

"There is only one time in my life that I asked another man for a favor," E. H. mused, "and he turned me down. It was on a hunting trip in Wyoming. We had run out of liquor and a man who was leaving had two bottles of whiskey. I asked him to sell me one of them and he refused."

I always felt like listening but E. H. did not feel like talking any more, and we trolled all morning and most of the afternoon with no excitement and very little conversation. Late in the afternoon we were opposite Cojímar, heading toward Havana, with the breeze kicking up a choppy sea, when the first large marlin of the season showed up on the surface, his purple side fins spread out like the wings of a huge bird, racing after the starboard teaser. There was no sound, no splash, no spray or sudden movement as we saw the long purple back of a 250-pound marlin sliding toward us down the side of a wave.

"*¡Adelante! ¡Adelante! ¡Más máquina!*" E. H. shouted to Carlos at the wheel, and the motor roared full speed ahead, E. H. racing in his bait and shouting orders in Spanish and Juan hauling in the teasers, with the marlin following them up to the stern. When the teasers were hauled on board, the fish charged the boat, evidently thinking the teasers were bonito that had taken refuge underneath; the marlin might have gone on into the propeller had E. H. not had the bait reeled in and dropped it on the fish's sword when the point of it was in the wash of the propeller, nearly touching the stern. The sword, head and shoulders of the marlin came out of the water and slashed sidewise at the bait. E. H., standing on the fish box above him, seeing that he had the bait well in his mouth and his jaws shut, struck immediately without slacking before he had a chance to jump and throw the hook. The fish suddenly disappeared, tearing line off the reel with a scream of metallic brakes straining against a terrific burst of speed, bending the rod like a buggy whip. Then he came up less than ten feet from the stern, flinging himself clear out of the water, dancing erect on his tail, shaking his head with his pointed jaws wide open, trying to throw the hook, his striped sides glistening silver in the late afternoon sun. He turned a somersault, went down in a splash of spray, came up again and again, throwing white spray in a rapid succession of somersaults. Every jump was a picture lost. I was paralyzed by the action. My bait was still out and by the time I had reeled in and opened the Graflex, the marlin sounded and headed for Havana in a run that kept the reel at a high-pitched shriek. E. H., sitting in the fishing chair with his feet braced against the side, screwed down the drag as tight as he could without snapping the line and tried to stop him.

"Get me the harness! The harness!" he said.

"Where is it?"

"In the locker, for chrissake!" Then to Carlos in Spanish, "Turn around! Turn around! Head toward Cojímar!"

Carlos, new to the wheel of a motor boat, did not turn her around. He kept the bow pointed seaward, believing the fish would head out to the stream where the water is seven hundred fathoms deep, the classic direction in which big fish make their run. He could not understand why E. H. wanted to go ashore.

"Turn around! Turn the boat around!" E. H. repeated.

Carlos still did not understand and, not understanding, did not obey. He used his own judgment.

"Turn the boat around or you take the rod and I'll take the wheel," E. H. said, using Spanish swearwords that have no English equivalents.

Carlos understood better when he saw the fish come up in five long, loping jumps three hundred yards directly astern, headed ashore toward Cojímar. The boat was hooked up fourteen knots an hour heading directly away from the fish. E. H. had seen the bellied line and knew this fish, an exception, was running toward shore. Being unable to fight the boat and the fish at the same time, he had lost almost all the five hundred yards of line while Carlos used his own judgment.

"Turn around! Turn around! Turn around! Follow the fish!" E. H. said desperately. "Can't anybody hold this chair, for chrissake?"

Carlos turned the boat and chased the marlin at an angle. I slipped the harness over Hemingway's shoulders and stood in back of him holding the chair to prevent it from turning. He went to work with all his might, pulling in the bellied line and pressing it tight against the felt handle with his thumbs in order to keep it from going out as he raised the bent rod slowly with both hands, reeling in rapidly as he lowered it, trying to get back what he had lost when Carlos made his run away from the fish.

With that much line out on the first run, all the odds were in the fish's favor; to make matters worse, the sea was rough and the sun was low in the west. It would soon be dark. Although it was cool, being so near sundown, E. H. soaked his shirt with sweat and when I got him a woolen sweater he soaked that, too. When his glasses fogged up, I cleaned them with toilet paper. Now that the jumping was over and the fish was fighting deep, all the visual action was in the boat and in the fisherman's struggle to pull up the line that pointed down into the water. For the rest of us, it was a period of strained tension—Carlos standing at the wheel excited and cussing himself, Juan bringing E. H. ice water to rinse his mouth, and me at his back, holding his chair. All we could do was wait while E. H. and the fish fought it out. He fought it for an hour with all the strain the bent rod would take without breaking tackle, and he had the spool refilled to the top of the reel soon after sunset, when it was beginning to get dark. The knot of the double line came out of the water and the whipped 250-pound striped marlin appeared on the surface, E. H. leading him to the stern and Carlos standing on the fish box with the big gaff, waiting for him to come within reach.

"Sharks!" E. H. exploded. "Bring the Mannlicher!"

Two big sharks, coming up from below, circled slowly beneath the marlin, closing in gradually, and the tired fish tried to get away. E. H. held him on a tight line, preventing him from starting another run but unable to bring him into the boat. I brought up the gun and E. H. shot into the water at the sharks. They were too deep to hit, but the explosion drove them down. E. H. had taken the rod and again begun to lead the fish toward the stern when the sharks came up a second time and circled around the marlin. The line went slack, cut off by one of the shark's fins in passing, and the marlin, with the hook in his mouth and the wire leader dragging, went down with the sharks after him.

E. H. cursed and reeled in quietly. He went below to take a sponge bath followed by a rubdown with alcohol, and changed into dry clothes as Carlos steered toward the lights of Havana. Nobody said anything as we ran in. Carlos had disgraced himself at the wheel by not taking orders, I had missed all the jumps and E. H. had lost his fish to a pair of sharks. Nobody was in a mood to talk.

I pondered all the cussing and excitement over a fish. I couldn't see it. What if the fish did take out all the line, break it and get away? No fortune lost! The meat wouldn't go over fifteen dollars. Peanuts compared to the investment in the boat. If it caused all this disgust and anger, why do it? For sport? That fish couldn't hurt anybody. It was nothing like riding a bronc. There the man is taking chances. He'll take a beating if he stays or is thrown, either way.

"You never want to get sore if I cuss you or talk hard to you when we're fighting a fish, because that doesn't mean a thing," E. H. said in the morning. "You ought to study Spanish so you could understand what I say to Carlos and Juan. You've got to cuss them or they won't think you're serious."

"I didn't get sore."

"If we'd had Josie* at the wheel, we would have landed that fish yesterday. It was just a case of abominable boat handling. When we lost all that line on the first run, it gave the sharks time to

---

* "Josie" here refers to Joe Russell, a Key West fisherman whose boat Hemingway used to rent for his fishing trips before he bought the *Pilar*. Joe Russell's own rumrunning adventures became partly those of E. H.'s own hero, Henry Morgan, in *To Have and Have Not*, the first part of which had been published as "One Trip Across" in *Cosmopolitan*, which so impressed the young Arnold Samuelson when he first read it that it caused him to journey to Key West to see E. H.

follow the scent. With this crew, I've got to fight the fish and steer the boat at the same time."

"What did Carlos do the other years?"

"He put on baits and handled the gaff."

"Was Josie good at the wheel?"

"The best I've ever seen. I never had to talk to him like I do these Cubans. He could judge the course of a fish through the water and he knew exactly where to put her. All I had to do was to fight the fish. Now I've got to run the boat, and if I don't cuss them loud enough they don't think I mean it.

"Why didn't Josie come along this year?"

"He couldn't afford it. He's making too much money selling beer to the sailors in Key West. I knew this is how it would turn out without him. Carlos has never handled the wheel in action before and he gets so excited he can't take orders. If we do hook into a really big fish this year, we'll lose him sure as hell."

16

Alphonso

COJO, THE MECHANIC, said he had a cousin named Alphonso who wanted to meet me because I was an American and he wanted to improve his English. He spoke Castilian Spanish, Cojo said, and it would be an advantageous aquaintance both ways.

Alphonso was nineteen years old and he weighed two hundred and fifty pounds. He had a small mouth, small black eyes, small ears and a tiny nose on a big round face and his thin hair was cut so short you could see his white scalp. I met him in the corner café one evening and he led me upstairs to the apartment where he lived and introduced me to his mother, who was as big as her son, and his father, a pilot. They were very hospitable Spaniards, and big eaters. Alphonso said he could eat two pounds of bread with bologna and cocoa for a late afternoon lunch and have a good appetite for supper. He said two pounds of bread was nothing for him.

"My brother, he says I eat too much," Alphonso said, "but I think he made a mistake for I never feel sick."

They lived in the second story of a big apartment building that had a square courtyard in the middle where the sun came through in the daytime; the children played on its tiles, while the women did their washing. Alphonso's room was on the street facing the harbor. He took me out to the narrow balcony above the sidewalk. I could see the *Pilar* at anchor with her lantern tied to the mast and Juan sitting in the stern, smoking his cigar. Alphonso was a student, therefore a revolutionary, and he showed me the bullet dents in the concrete wall and began telling me of the part he had played in the overthrow of the Machado government.

"I do not know how many I killed, but I shoot many times," he said. "I am a member of the ABC. We are very strong, very powerful, and we have much ammunition, many guns. You see there across the street? There were many soldiers there with seven machine guns, no? They were waiting behind sandbags because they heard some ABC was going to put a bomb on the streetcar tracks there. It was in the time of the revolution. I had a Thompson gun. It is a very good gun, no? Very effective. It shoots many times. I have my orders. I went up on the top of the roof and I could see over the wall down on the soldiers, but they could not see me. I shot down at them, bum, bum, bum, many times and I know I hit two because I saw one limp and one fell over when they run away. That is what they always do. They run away when somebody shoots. They left their seven machine guns and run as fast as they could for more help. There was a cistern tank of water on the roof. I dropped my Thompson gun in the water, and when I went down the stairs to the courtyard the people had heard the shooting and they were running into their rooms with their backs turned so nobody saw me come down. I went into my room and washed my hands good and sat down reading a book. Then many soldiers came upstairs with their rifles to take this fellow who shoot from the roof. Nobody else was on the roof and nobody saw me come down. The soldiers came into all the rooms and they asked to see my hands. They were very clean, they had no powder marks or smell because I had washed them with soap and I explained I was reading the book when I hear this shooting. There are so many people in this house the soldiers could not discover who it was, they could not find the gun and they could not take us all to prison, so they had to go away. Very good, no?"

"And what about the gun?"

"I sold it afterward for ten dollars. It was too dangerous to keep."

"How old were you?"

"Seventeen."

"Pretty young, weren't you?"

"No. I was a captain of the ABC. Many other revolutionaries were much younger than me. I can tell you many things about the revolution. Very interesting, no?"

Alphonso, enormously fat and good-natured, certainly did not look like a killer. I thought the reason he was so eager to tell about his experience on the roof was that he was built very much like a woman and he wanted to assert himself as a man.

"How many knots makes that boat?" he asked, looking down at the *Pilar*.

"About fourteen."

"Very good boat for an expedition, no? She could carry many arms from the United States, no?"

"I'd never thought of that."

"Oh, yes. She can run much faster than the government boats. It would be very easy. With this boat I could make plenty money."

"Pretty dangerous business, isn't it?"

"For me, no. If they catch me, I tell them 'You know who am I? I am a member of the ABC. If you kill me they will kill you.' Oh, yes, we are very strong, very powerful organization. They would not dare to kill me. But I would not get caught. How do you like Havana?"

"Swell."

"I hope you can stay for the next revolution."

"We'll be here three months."

"Then you will see plenty."

"We've already heard a few bombs go off downtown from the boat."

"That is nothing. It is only the Communists. They are very broke and they have no money to buy bombs. When the ABCs start, you will see something."

"Who's at the head of the ABCs?"

"No one knows. Not even the members. It is a very secret organization but very powerful. Oh, yes. We are very powerful."

"Do you have revolutions all the time?"

"Always bombs on the streets. Big fighting, no, because it takes too much time to get expeditions of dynamite and rifles from the States, and we must get the soldiers to turn to our side. Then when it is time we strike."

"Why?"

"Our government officials get too rich robbing the poor and we want to throw them out and get new ones."

"When you get new ones, why don't you keep them?"

"Because soon they start to rob the poor like the old ones."

"Aren't there any honest officials?"

"Maybe some when they go in, because they never had a chance to rob, but when they are in power they all turn crooked to make money."

"Then, what's the use?"

"I cannot say. We hope for an intervention of the United States. We cannot govern but we can revolt."

Just then we heard three voices in hot argument from the kitchen. I did not want to embarrass Alphonso by overhearing the family row, but he led me into the other room so he could take part in it. El Cojo and Alphonso's father were arguing with Alphonso's mother and their voices were so loud and excited I expected the argument would turn into a fistfight.

"It is about the passenger bus," Alphonso explained. "My mother, she says it runs on one street and we say it runs on a different street. It used to run where she says, not now. It has changed. We know because we see it every day but you cannot make her believe."

"Why doesn't she see for herself?"

"She is afraid to go outside. She has not been outside of the house for two years. You cannot make her go outside. She is afraid of the shooting on the streets. There is too much revolution."

The men dropped the discussion and Alphonso's mother became the quiet, good-natured old woman again, satisfied that she had had the best of the argument.

"Would you care to take a walk?" I asked Alphonso.

"Okay, come on, let's go," he answered. "Where did you want to go? Do you like to see some gals?"

Alphonso put on a hat to cover his short haircut and ran ahead of me down the stairs four steps at a stride.

"You'll break your neck doing that!"

"I fell only once," he said, when we were on the street. "I received many injuries, no? But I break nothing."

"Better take it easy."

"Oh, I shall not fall again. Where do you like to go? You like to see some gals?"

"Let's go down to the Prado."

"I know many places. They all know who am I. I was a captain in the revolution. We were hunting for the officers of Machado's army who were hiding in the whorehouses. It was very good entertainment. Very funny. I came in with my revolutionaries. We are heavily armed. We have to search every room and we could not wait and give the officers a chance to escape."

"Did you find any officers?"

"No. But we find many customers. Very good entertainment. Some of the houses are very big, no? They have more than one hundred gals. The owners get very angry because when we are there nobody can leave and nobody can come in. It spoils business. They say to me, 'We will pay you anything if you will take your men away.' But no, we are revolutionaries. We are after officers, not money. We must search every room, and we find the customers."

"Are there many houses in Havana?"

"Very many. It is a very good business, no?"

"How much do they charge?"

"Anything you wish to pay. Twenty-five cents and up. You can get a good clean gal for fifty cents. If you are an American, they charge you twice as much. Some Americans pay as high as twenty-five dollars. They have very fine clothes, very fine apartments, everything very fine, but it is the same stuff."

"Why are these windows boarded?"

"Somebody threw a bomb."

We had gone by the Ambos Mundos Hotel on our way toward the Prado, and I noticed many of the display windows of the business buildings were broken out and covered with plywood.

"But there are so many. You'd think it was an earthquake."

"No. All bombs. That is the reason the merchants want American intervention. Revolutionaries need money and if the merchant will not pay, he gets a bomb."

"Can't the police do anything?"

"The policemen throw, too, many bombs. Many are Communists. It is very easy for them. They throw a bomb when nobody is looking and then they begin shooting down the street. They telephone headquarters and they say a big car came by and threw the bomb. They shoot but it escaped before they could see the license number. It works very good, no?"

"It must."

"It is really dangerous to walk on the streets at night. You do not know when they are going to throw a bomb. If you are in the way, that makes no difference. Many have been killed at one time. I have seen it many times but I have been very lucky. I really think there will be some shooting tonight. I can feel it. You don't see many people on the streets. That is a bad sign. If you hear any shooting, don't run. That is the most foolish thing you can do, because if you run they think you are trying to escape and they shoot you down. If you hear some shooting, just walk as we are walking now until you have a chance to get in someplace."

"Are you afraid?"

"Me? No! If the soldiers take me I will tell them, 'You do not know who am I? I am a member of the ABC.' They are afraid for their lives so they will let me go."

We strolled along under the bright lights of the Prado, and a Cuban who spotted me as an American walked beside me and began telling me about a place he knew where there were many beautiful healthy sixteen-year-old girls. I told him I was too tired, married, devoted and faithful to my wife, did not feel like it, did not care especially for his company and that we were meeting our wives and preferred not being seen with a pimp, but I could not insult him or get rid of him. I had met so many of his kind in Havana that it began to appear the logical profession for a Cuban who could speak English well enough to be understood. Several had followed me for ten blocks or more, and this one began to get me worried. I was afraid to hit him because I was in a foreign country.

"You have had enough of this fellow, no?" Alphonso said.

"Enough is right."

Alphonso spoke a few words of Spanish and the pimp dropped back.

"What did you tell him?"

"I know that place very well. They have no young girls there.

They are all as old as my grandmother. They make you drunk and take your money away from you and then they throw you out on the street. It is a dangerous place. I know them all."

Alphonso showed me many places. Prostitution was the business that opened at night when the others closed. We walked by one building that extended the length of the block, with doors only ten feet apart, held half open by chains on the inside and with a woman sitting at every door in the dim light. Some of them said "Pssst! Come on, boy," as we went by. There were many young women in that block and some very good-looking ones, I thought, but Alphonso said it was all cheap stuff. He preferred a Mexican gal who had a place on another street. We went to her door, but found it locked; then we went to another house, where Alphonso walked off with a tall brunette. I waited for him in the lobby, where a girl sat at the doorway with her legs opened carelessly, watching the street and saying "Pssst!" whenever she saw a man pass by on the sidewalk. There were two other men in the waiting room, a soldier and a well-dressed young man who kept his eyes on the girl. After a while he led her off and another girl took her place at the door.

"Why did you not take a gal?" Alphonso asked me when we were on the street again. "Did not you like that stuff?"

"I'm afraid of getting a dose."

"It is no danger. I go here often and I only had gonorrhea one time."

"Why are there so many whores in Havana?"

"It is a good business, no?"

"But why do they do it?"

"It is better than to not take food."

"You mean they have to do that so they won't starve?"

"Yes. Life is very hard in Havana."

I thought about his two pounds of bread and bologna for lunch.

"It must be pretty tough," I said.

"It is tough. I feel sorry for the Mexican gal. That is why I usually go to her. She tells me even now she goes some days without taking food, and I believe her because she is very thin. She supports a young daughter, who stays with other people and does not know what her mother is doing. She has a very hard life."

We turned a corner, and Alphonso saw the Mexican gal's door was open.

"She is there now," he said. "It is really too bad. I should have waited. She needs the money."

"How much do you pay her?"

"Fifty cents. Never pay more than fifty cents. That is all it is worth."

17

The Phony Fisherman

WE TROLLED ten days without seeing a fish, even though all the signs known to fishermen were favorable. The current was strong close into shore, the breeze was from the northeast, the moon was right and it was the time of year for the biggest run of the season, yet the sea was apparently empty. The market fishermen said they had been catching a few on their handlines at a depth of two hundred fathoms, but none of them had seen any marlin traveling on the surface, nor had Rico, captain of a charter yacht, nor had the owner of the fishing yacht *Siboney.* Every morning we went out early and trolled all day through the empty dark-blue waves without seeing a fish of any kind except the sharks in the garbage, and every night when we came in, tired and disappointed, E. H. was told that a man nicknamed the Príncipe, or "Prince of the Fishermen," had brought another marlin into the Havana Yacht Club to be photographed. The Príncipe, son of a wealthy American tobacco manufacturer, certainly did not look like a marlin fisherman. He was soft and fat, and it was said of him that he had hit a whore in a whorehouse and when another customer was about to interfere had lain down on the floor and said, "Don't hit me. I'm a cripple." In the mornings, we used to see the Príncipe in the harbor showing off the speed of his motorboat, which had its stern built so high above his fishing chair it would break his rod if a fish fought deep close to the boat, yet he came in early in the forenoons, always with a good-sized marlin, and we stayed out all day and saw nothing. At night the Príncipe liked to drink in the expensive cafés and tell about how easy it was for him to catch a fish. He was surprised that E. H. was having such bad luck.

"What size tackle do you use?" E. H. asked him one evening.

"Eighteen-ounce rod. Sixteen-thread line."

"I couldn't do it. I'm using thirty-six thread."

"Lately, I've been using twenty-four."

"I couldn't do that, either," E. H. said. "Not in that depth of water."

"I admit it is rather difficult with the lighter tackle," the Príncipe said. "Still, my luck has been rather above average. At the Havana Yacht Club, they will tell you I've brought in fifteen in the last two weeks and not one under two hundred pounds. One weighed three twenty. Here are the pictures."

"Very remarkable," E. H. said. "We don't even see them."

On our way out to the stream the next morning we met the Príncipe already coming in with a 350-pound marlin laid across his bow.

"How do you like this one?" he yelled as the boats met head on and passed nearly touching.

"Swell! Where did you buy it?" E. H. shouted back.

The Príncipe opened his mouth in a blank stare of astonishment and made no reply as his boat fell astern in our wake, headed for Havana. He was sitting in the fishing chair, surrounded by beautiful women, holding the rod with his heavy leather harness fastened to the reel. He wore a clean white shirt and his face was covered with white powder to protect it from the sun. At first I thought he had turned white when E. H. asked him where he bought the fish.

"I said it without thinking," E. H. said. "I don't know just what it is but the whole damned layout strikes me as phony. If he had hooked into a fish in this sun, he would have sweated that powder off his face and that white shirt of his would be wringing wet. No fisherman would wear that hot leather harness any longer than he had to. If his crew had hauled a fish on board, they'd have left it on the deck. They'd have been too tired to carry it up across the bow. It's the phoniest setup I've ever seen."

Carlos said it was a serious thing to charge a sportsman with having bought a fish unless you had proof.

"All right, then, we'll get proof or apologize and I'm damned

Arnold Samuelson in his senior year as a journalism major at the University of Minnesota. Below, with Hemingway on the deck of the Pilar.

"E. H. was happy at the wheel. It was a beautiful, clear day, and he was going out for the sport he loved in the best fishing grounds in the world at the wheel of his own boat, which was built just as he had wanted her built..."

"Juan made a reputation for himself with [this] meal. He served five dishes of Pauline's marlin meat prepared in five different ways, each a masterpiece."

"What impressed me most was Hemingway's incredible eyesight. He sometimes saw the fish take the bait and told us what it was before the man at the rod knew he had a strike, or if he happened to be looking ahead when the fish struck and sounded, he could tell by the way it pulled what sort of a fish and how big it was."

The _Pilar_ putting out to sea in the Havana harbor.

"When Gattorno was happy, he felt like singing and beating time on the fish box with his fists, and there was no stopping him. E. H. said he was the youngest man he knew."

"I had never seen E. H. so pleased to see anybody as his friend Sidney Franklin, the great matador. The man in the brown suit wearing a black beret on the side of his head, with a blond Jewish face and aggressive manners... seemed to be the one man he completely admired."

'Lillian Gattorno had never thought that there might be a difficulty in getting into the movies. She thought the railway fare to Hollywood was all that stood in the way of her becoming a star, and once she got there it would be easy."

"They started up a rousing Spanish song, singing it with the abandonment of drunkards feeling marvelous, none of them having had a drink yet, E. H. joining in with a lusty bass."

"E. H. was feeling marvelous up there in the bow with the harpoon gun, while we moved at a slow trolling speed...He knew by hearsay what danger we would be in if a wounded whale tried to knock the <u>Pilar</u> out of the sea...and with all the life belts gone with the hurricane rope it would be a long swim three miles to shore..."

"Some years later the porpoises of that day appeared in the dream of the fisherman in <u>The Old Man and the Sea</u>. 'He did not dream of lions but instead of a vast school of porpoises that stretched for eight or ten miles and it was the time of their mating and they would leap high into the air and return to the same hole they made in the water when they leaped.'"

Ernest Hemingway, Lopez Mendez, Carlos and Arnold with a 250-pound silver marlin hung up to be weighed at Cabañas fortress. Seen in close up and (below) from a distance.

Arnold, Carlos, Pauline, Juan, Cadwalader and E. H. showing head and bill of a 324-pound blue marlin.

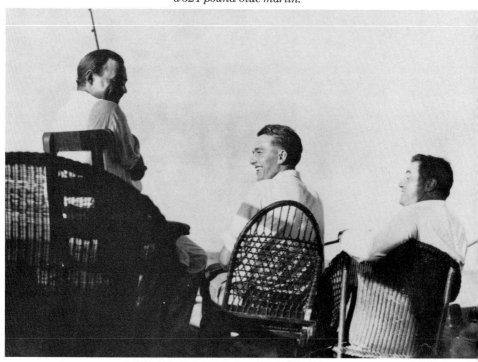

"The old wicker chairs... used to slide around the deck and sometimes tip over in the rough seas. I compared the old chairs to bucking broncs, and E. H. said, 'When I was in Wyoming, they asked what I did for a living and I told them I was a writer. They thought I said rider. I've never been able to ride a horse.'"

sure I'm not going to apologize. This is something we've got to investigate because if that son of a bitch is buying little fish he's got plenty of money, and he'll naturally buy big fish when they're caught, and what's stopping him from claiming a world's record with rod and reel?"

The phony had to be shown up.

The market fishermen would leave Havana early in the morning before daylight, when the sea was calm, and row out to the stream and drift with the current until the breeze made the water too rough for their little boats and they had to raise the sails at their bows and come in along the countercurrent near shore. Carlos, the oldest of the market fishermen, was their leader. E. H. had met the fisherman one winter when Carlos was captain of a Cuban smack fishing off Dry Tortugas, near Key West. Carlos had told him about the marlin, and the next summer, with Carlos as his guide, E. H. became the first sportsman to fish marlin with rod and reel in Cuban waters. The market fishermen, amused at first and thinking it could not be done with such light tackle, were amazed when E. H. caught sixty in a season while they were lucky to kill ten. E. H. was not a competitor, the fishermen being interested only in the marlin feeding deep. They liked E. H. because he gave them the sharks he caught, if there was a skiff near, and he always ran within shouting distance to exchange fishing news.

That morning we saw them out in the stream, two men in every boat, three miles from shore, tossing up on the waves and dropping out of sight in the troughs, one man at the oars, keeping the boat nosed into the sea, his partner at the bow holding the handlines. E. H. put the *Pilar* full speed ahead and ran from one skiff to another, asking the fishermen if they had seen a motor cruiser fighting a marlin that morning. They said the motorboat had come by and asked them if they had any fish, but they had not seen it in action. Only one marlin had been killed, a Cojímar fisherman had killed it, and he had raised his sail and gone in. E. H. hooked up both motors and headed for Cojímar. There he found and took pictures of the two market fishermen who admitted they had sold the Príncipe his 350-pound marlin for twenty-two dollars.

Meanwhile the Príncipe returned to the Havana Yacht Club, hung up the marlin and took several photographs of himself and the fish before an admiring audience. His admirers later kept telephoning him at all hours of the night to ask how much he had really paid for the marlin. We never saw the Príncipe boat out after that. His folks were afraid that Hemingway would use the incident to brighten up one of his *Esquire* pieces, but E. H. said, "Why waste that stuff on an article? I might want to put it in a story sometime."

"What! You are twenty-two years old and you do not know how to make a bomb?" Alphonso said to me one evening. "What do they teach you in the United States of America?"

"We don't use many bombs over there," I said.

"It is really very easy, very simple. Here we all know how to make a bomb. I will teach you."

"Thanks, but I don't think I'd have much use for it."

"You never can tell," he said. "When you go back to the States it might be very handy. It is really easy. A piece of pipe and a stick of dynamite is all you need. You can blow up anything."

"What would I blow up?"

"Anything you do not like."

"What have you blown up?"

"One time I blew up a general of Machado's army."

Alphonso's mother was making hot chocolate and a tortilla of sliced bananas mixed with six beaten eggs, seasoned with salt and pepper and fried in olive oil. There were three loaves of Cuban bread, a yard long and three inches wide, on the table, as well as a kettle of garbanzos and a big platter of marlin meat. Alphonso always liked to have a lunch late in the evening when we returned from our walks downtown, and, the meals being so frequent in his house, the food was never cleared off the table.

"I am a member of the ABCs," Alphonso said. "It is a very powerful organization. If you do not do what they say, they will kill you. If they tell a member to throw a bomb at his own house, he has to do it or he will be shot. That is why we are very powerful, no?

"This general had made his soldiers to shoot one of the ABCs. The next day we discovered he had ordered a pair of boots from a factory. We made a package with a bomb inside with a flashlight battery fixed so the wires would touch when the package was opened. I met the messenger from the factory and I said to him 'Do you have the boots for the general?' He says 'Yes.' 'Very well,' I say. 'I'm from the general. How much money?' I gave him thirty dollars and I took the other package to the clerk of the hotel and I said

'Here are the boots for the general.' The bellboy brought the package up to the general's room and a few minutes afterward the whole building shook with a great big boom! They found the general scattered all over the ceiling. Very good, no?"

"Can your mother understand what we say?"

"No. She does not understand English."

"Then what happened?"

"Then the ABC get really busy. Everybody in Havana knows about it. We found out Machado was going to have a big military funeral for the general. All the big shots would be there, so this was the chance to clean up. We get very busy at night and dig a tunnel in the cemetery near the open grave for the general and we fill it full of many hundred pounds of dynamite and we set a clock so it will go off at the time of the funeral. There are two cemeteries close to each other and at the last minute Machado decided to have the general buried in the other cemetery. That spoiled everything. Machado and all his big officers were standing at the grave, waiting for the soldiers to shoot over the coffin, when they hear the explosion, and at the other cemetery they see the gravestones flying up into the air. If they had not changed their minds, we would have cleaned up the Machado government in one blow.

"The chocolate is ready. Let us eat. This tortilla is for you. She will make one other for me. Take some garbanzos. Take some meat. Take more bread. You have nothing. Eat more. Eat plenty. Eat!"

18

Coming in at Cabañas

THE NEXT TIME Pauline came over we loaded heavily with ice, beer and food and left the harbor early in the morning, heading against the current, close in to the Havana shore, for a cruise up the Cuban coast. There was a sort of holiday spirit on board that made it different from the other days, when we fished over the usual route down the stream in the morning and back at night. That day we were traveling to new fishing grounds, to a place I had never seen before, and we were not coming back that night. Both motors were humming, the boat moving swiftly over the flat sea, the phonograph playing popular records and the teasers dancing gracefully on top of the water in time with the music. Pauline, Lopez and I held the rods. E. H. was at the wheel, where he had a better view of the changing scenery as we passed the big buildings of Havana and came to the outlying cottages along the beach, in a few minutes reaching the apparently uninhabited, brush-covered green coast he said looked exactly like the coast of Africa—and he wished he was back. If he ever quit the writing racket he could make his living there as a guide, and if he had this boat on the African coast there would be big money in taking parties out swordfishing. It would be a damned sight easier than writing.

The level green behind the white strip of sand became higher as we continued up the coast, and toward noon we began to see a few royal palms, less brush and more palms on the hills. We saw a sailfish jump eight times, trying to shake off his suckerfish, and a small marlin followed the baits for a while but went down without striking. He was not hungry, merely playing, E. H. said. Lopez caught a five-pound tuna, which Juan fried for lunch, serving it with avocados, lobster salad, spaghetti, sliced pineapple and Castilian wine. While we were eating, Lopez Mendez spoke of his wife and Antonio, his friend, who had run off with her.

"There were all the other women in the world and he had to take her," he said. "If he had not gone away, I think maybe I would have killed him, and then I would have to stay two years in jail, maybe more."

"A son of a bitch like that ought to be killed," E. H. said.

"But it would only get me into trouble."

"I'll kill him for you," E. H. offered as a favor. "I wouldn't feel bad about it. I've killed a lot of men. He'd be easy. He isn't afraid of me and if we could get him out on the boat, who the hell could prove he didn't fall overboard? But we couldn't use this crew. I'd get Josie. He knows how to keep his mouth shut."

"But Antonio is in Mexico now."

"He might come back."

"I don't see what she could see in him," Pauline said.

116

"I think maybe she soon will be tired of him," Lopez answered. "In six months maybe she will want to come back."

"Would you take her back?"

"Never. I am getting my divorce. I should like very much to marry an American girl. I like Ginger Rogers very well."

It clouded over early in the afternoon, and in the dull light that penetrated the dark clouds we saw the opening in the land that marked the entrance to Cabañas harbor and headed in through the curved channel filled with blue Gulf water, which widened into a big muddy lake fringed with mangroves on the low shore and on the islands, the lake reaching to the foot of the round mountains ahead that were covered with royal palms. This was different from anything we had seen near Havana, and we went forward to get the feeling of the tropics, which was intensified by the ragged shoreline closed in with green mangroves, brush and the forests of leaning palm trees spotting the sides of the mountains and standing against the gray sky and the green smell of the mangroves and the stagnant water, which lay so flat you would think it had never been touched. The boat glided ahead smoothly, and we could feel and hear the accentuated throb and wash of the propeller and the vibration and sound of the big motor on an easy pull while we sat in the bow, looking, listening, smelling and sensing the tropics with very little talking.

We traveled three or four miles across the lake to the small town of Cabañas at the foot of the mountain and tied to the low pier, where the barefooted men and naked children had gathered to see the boat. Going ashore, we took a path up a hill past huts built of palm branches, with open doors and windows and no furniture of any kind to be seen inside. We stopped at the top of the hill at an old concrete house with bars across the windows where the town delegate lived and E. H. presented the boat's papers. The delegate's son, a market fisherman, gave E. H. the sword of an 800-pound marlin that had towed his skiff three miles out to sea before he could kill it. E. H. invited the youth on board, and with him at the wheel we took a trip into a mangrove swamp through a winding channel which looked like a river that had stopped running, banked with tall and impenetrable green mangroves growing out of the shallow water with oysters attached to their forked roots. Many times we had to dodge overhanging branches and at the curves the boat scraped against the brush. The channel was alive with small fish jumping, alligators and many different kinds of birds. It led into an open lagoon in the center of the swamp, and after we were in there we could never have found our way out without our guide because there were so many blind openings that looked like the channel, and they all looked alike.

We headed back toward Cabañas as the sun was setting and the clouds were breaking. We put the young fisherman ashore and Carlos, heading the *Pilar* out toward the lagoon, ran her onto a sandbank. All hands jumped overboard in the dark to push her back off, standing waist deep in the warm water and straining against the sides of the boat, which had never looked so big before, while E. H. was running the propeller backward. She came off at last and we ran out to the middle of the lagoon, where there were no mosquitoes, to anchor for the night.

We were sitting in the cockpit after supper, drinking cognac and listening to the phonograph, when we saw a rowboat start out from shore carrying a lantern at the bow. We watched the lantern light come toward us through the darkness and could see the native rowing in the bow and the two soldiers sitting with their rifles raised across their chests. The soldiers came on board with their rifles; one had Chinese eyes and the taller one had a flat nose and thick lips. They said they were stationed at the old fortress at the mouth of the harbor which we had believed to be abandoned and were on guard for ships smuggling arms for the revolutionaries. E. H. showed them the ship's papers, which they appeared unable to read, and said they were welcome to search the ship but first they ought to have a drink. He gave them each a glass of *coñac francés,* which they swallowed at a gulp, and poured them Castilian wine and whiskey cocktails. The soldiers, finding themselves in such agreeable company, did not feel like asking questions or searching the boat. They were in no hurry to go back to their solitary post, where they saw natives once a week and outsiders perhaps once a year. They felt more like sitting on the fish box, listening to E. H. talk about Africa. E. H. entertained them for two hours, and when they reluctantly stepped back into the boat and rowed ashore he had them cinched. They might come on board to visit again but they would never search the ship. If E. H. wanted to haul a load of dynamite, it would be safe to come in at Cabañas harbor.

Lopez slept out on the cockpit and was the first one up. While

Carlos mopped the dew off the roof and Juan made coffee, Lopez fished a handline over the side and caught thirteen blue runners from a school that swarmed out from underneath the boat to examine his sardine baits. It was a bright morning, with the sun shining on the hills and the lagoon, and we felt like going in for a swim but decided not to when we saw a shark's fin moving slowly not far from the boat. After breakfast we pulled up the anchor and headed out toward the sea in the bright morning sunlight. The clear Gulf water was far into the channel and we could see the fish swimming deep down past the dark patches of marine growth at the bottom, which became darker and dimmer as we moved on into deeper water until they were lost in the purple. Carlos headed out far enough to take advantage of the full strength of the current and set a straight course for Havana. Lopez caught an eight-pound dog shark, Pauline caught a wahoo and I caught a barracuda. We did not see any marlin and we came in at Havana harbor early in the afternoon and went ashore.

The next time Hemingway came on board he brought a manuscript envelope with my own handwriting on it that had been sent back by *Field and Stream.*

"Now for chrissake don't let that discourage you," E. H. said. "That's to be expected. It doesn't mean a damned thing when they send them back. Sometimes the magazines have bought up stuff for months ahead and they can't buy anything. There are so many other factors involved it isn't necessarily a reflection on a writer if they don't take his stuff. I sent articles on bullfights to every magazine I could think of, and they all sent them back. They'd be willing to pay plenty for them now. You don't want to let that get you down. You'll get something better later on. There hasn't been anything to write yet, because we haven't run into any fish. This year has been as disastrous for fishing as it was up North for the crops. The run should start any time now. I'd been hoping we'd hook into a record marlin, because then you'd have something they'd almost have to take."

19

Bumby and the Storyteller

WE HAD HEARD E. H. talk so much about his friend Sidney Franklin, the great matador, and we had been expecting him for such a long time that we were very anxious to meet him. On the first of August, the day he came across, we went out to meet the *Cuba* and ran alongside the big ship as she headed into Havana. E. H. tried to find Sidney among the passengers standing along the rail, and when he saw the man in the brown suit wearing a black beret on the side of his head, he put his hands together around his mouth and yelled, "Hi, Sid!"

"Hi, Ernest!" the man yelled back.

"We'll anchor at the fishing dock!"

"At the fishing dock!" Sidney nodded his head to show that he understood.

Soon after we had anchored, Sidney came out on a motor launch and climbed on board. He was full of confidence, and shook hands vigorously with E. H. I had never seen E. H. so pleased to see anybody. This bullfighter with a blond Jewish face and aggressive manners seemed to be the one man he completely admired. I could not understand that admiration, because I had never seen Sidney in front of a bull. E. H. had traveled the bullfight circuit through Spain with him, when Sidney was going good. In the last fight, he had seen the bull pick up Sidney, carry him on his horns and toss him into the air; he had been there when they carried Sidney screaming out of the ring into the infirmary.

"You're looking bloody marvelous," E. H. told Sidney.

"Hell, I feel swell, Ernest."

"You look three hundred percent better than last time I saw you. I never thought you'd come out of it, but you're looking damned marvelous. The only thing is your fanny still sticks out too much."

"The hell it does. Joan Crawford told me I had a damned good figure and that means something, coming from her."

"Christ, I'm glad to see you looking so well, Sid. How is everybody in Hollywood?"

"Charlie Chaplin is a hell of a swell fellow. You'd like him, Ernest. Those movie stars are damned swell people when you come in riding on the top as I did, so you can get acquainted with them. I had a hell of a good time."

"How about that picture?" E. H. asked.

"They called it *The Kid from Spain.* I worked the bulls for Eddie Cantor in the bullfight scene. They used four different bulls for the same scene."

E. H. repeated what Sidney had said in Spanish for Carlos and Juan and they laughed loudly, having waited for a chance to let out their feelings while they watched every gesture of the great matador, their hero, who paid no attention to them. Then Sidney spoke in Spanish, in the rich buzzing Spanish spoken by Cojo and Juan. That left me out, and I could only listen to their voices. The dark eyes of Carlos and Juan lighted with pleasure as they overheard what was said, and Juan, with a loose smile on his mouth, asked Sidney a question. Sidney cut him short with a sharp retort that took the smile off Juan's lips. It was intended to keep Juan in his place, and it did.

"How did you like the country around Hollywood?" I asked Sidney.

"What the hell do you care?" he answered, keeping *me* in my place.

The next day when he went out fishing with us, Sidney's manners had changed and I understood E. H. had talked to him. Sidney told us about his most interesting experiences with bulls and women and was very entertaining.

Pauline had come over with Bumby, who was becoming a he-man under his father's supervision with the boxing gloves and fishing rods, and her cousin, Ward Meriner, a short, young college graduate who had majored in Greek and was soon telling me the adventures of Alcibiades, an Athenian general in the Peloponnesian War. Bumby had to stay on board all the time, not being allowed to go ashore on account of the epidemic of infantile paralysis, and Ward and I used to entertain him in the cockpit until his bedtime.

Ernest had bought him a hunting knife, and when he was bored with poking holes in the sun goggles, he would say, "Tell me a story."

"Once there was a guy called Daniel Boone," Ward would begin.

"I know all about him," Bumby would say. "Tell me another one."

"Well, then, how about Buffalo Bill?"

"I know all about him, too. Tell me something different."

"Ever hear about Robinson Crusoe, the guy who lived on an island?"

"Yes. I've read the book."

"Ever read your father's books?"

"No. They're too grown up for me. Tell me a story."

"I know one about a guy called Jesse James."

"So do I."

"Tell him a Greek one," I suggested.

"Did you ever hear about Alcibiades?" Ward asked.

"Not that I can remember. Tell me about him."

Ward gave an account of the Greek hero's life, leaving out the love affairs, and at last Bumby was satisfied. Ward's classical background came in very handy.

At nine o'clock we told Bumby to go to bed, and when Juan came on board we went downtown to drink beer at the tables on the sidewalk of the Prado, across from the Capitolio, and listen to the Cuban orchestra playing American jazz. We were the only ones there wearing nothing over our shirts, and the waiters would not have served us if they had not known we were Americans. We sat drinking our beers and watching the dressed-up Cubans at the other tables. We did not feel ill at ease in our shirts because we were Americans.

"Has Ernest ever told you what he thinks of me?" I asked Ward.

"No, but that's quite a coincidence," Ward said.

"Why?"

"Ernest asked me the same thing about you."

"What did you say?"

"I told him you had never said anything about it."

"What did he say?"

"He said he thinks you want to be his pal, but he doesn't want any pals. He said he used to have pals but he had too many disappointments."

"What more did he say?"

"He said humanity could be divided into two classes, the bastards and the son of a bitches."

"Is that all?"

"No. He told me to bring more money the next time I come."

20

A Fish for the Scientificos

WE WERE WAITING for the scientificos. Marlin had never been classified scientifically, and E. H. was disgusted with the reports of fishermen who were constantly discovering and naming new species. E. H. did not believe the so-called white marlin, striped marlin, silver marlin, blue marlin, black marlin and the giant Tahitian black marlin were different species. He believed they were growth stages and sex and color variations of the same fish. The colors had never been scientifically described because the ichthyologists had only studied them after they were killed and brought in on the dock, by which time their colors had disappeared. In a letter to C. M. B. Cadwalader, director of the Philadelphia Academy of Natural History, E. H. suggested he send an ichthyologist to Havana to study the marlin from the *Pilar* and see the colors of the fish alive in the water. He wanted them scientifically described and classified so that fishermen could identify their catches and know what they were talking about. Cadwalader agreed to send his man down and offered to come himself and pay half the gas. E. H. told him he did not take paying guests but he was welcome to come and fish for ten days, and suggested the gasoline money be used to keep the ichthyologist in Havana for a month so he would be sure to see a variety of fish. E. H. told him to come by the end of July, probably the time of the biggest run this year.

E. H. met the scientificos at the hotel the night they came, and it was not until the next morning that we saw them, when they were walking down toward the dock, E. H. between them, so much bigger he looked like a father with two sons. One of them had white hair and the stiff-jointed walk of a man beginning to get old; the other, middle-aged and shorter, carried a big fishing rod and walked with his head back and his arms swinging stiff at the elbows. They came out on the dock and stood on the edge waiting for Carlos to reach them in the *Bumby*. They stepped carefully into the boat while Carlos held her against the pier and sat down holding onto the sides. Carlos shoved the *Bumby* clear and rowed standing up, pushing the oars ahead of his chest.

"I venture to say that we will encounter a marlin today," the short man was saying as they came coasting alongside the *Pilar*.

"Hell, yes," E. H. said. "We'll get one."

"You cannot imagine what this really means to me. I have never had the opportunity to fish marlin before and I anticipate a great deal of pleasure."

"Hell, yes," E. H. said. "You'll get your bellyful if they start running."

The white-haired man said nothing. He was Henry Fowler, the ichthyologist; the short man was Charles Cadwalader, his boss, and out of politeness he let him talk to E. H. first.

Cadwalader, short-legged, slightly pot-bellied, always wore the same club-room conversationalist expression on his freckled face, and when he talked to one person he spoke as if he were making a speech to a crowd or speaking for the benefit of those who might be trying to overhear, like a lecturer answering questions of people in his audience. They talked about the waterfront sights as we headed out into the stream, and E. H. showed Cadwalader how to hold the spool loose with his hand when we let the baits over and began fishing.

"I had been planning a hunting expedition to Africa, but the way business conditions are now I really can't afford it," Cadwalader said.

"What's the matter?" I asked. "Doesn't the museum pay you much?"

Cadwalader was insulted. "Oh, no! I receive no remuneration whatever. Entirely gratis. As a matter of fact, it is largely through my contributions that the institution is able to continue. I've built it up to what it is, as a matter of fact."

"Then what are you worried about?"

"The present economic outlook being what it is, you have no assurance whatever."

I had not yet been told that this bachelor philanthropist was the last of a distinguished line of money-making, money-hoarding Cadwaladers. It was not until later that I was told he kept twenty-seven servants in his house and was very much upset because an old woman intended to retire and it would be like losing one of the parts in a smooth-running machine. This was the first man I had run into who had so many ancestors and so much money, and I had difficulty understanding him. He would not drink vermouth with us before dinner or wine with his meals or whiskey in the evenings, but would only drink bottled mineral water, and half the mornings he forgot to bring his mineral water and E. H. would have to send Juan ashore for it before we could leave. Cadwalader never gave Juan any money. He must be worried about his investments, I thought. He had to spend so many thousands to keep the museum going and as an economy measure he let E. H. pay for his mineral water.

The white-haired ichthyologist brought out the pieces of a net and screwed the segments of the handle together. He dipped up patches of seaweed and shook out little fish half-an-inch long, which he dropped in a jar of alcohol. Juan thought that was a lot of fun. He asked to try, and spent hours sitting in the bow in the afternoons when he had nothing else to do, with the net ready to capture the tiny forms of marine life hiding under the seaweed; when he made a catch he would come running with the quarter-inch fish flipping in the palm of his hand, shouting, *"¡Mira!* Look at the scientific fish! Maybe it is a small marlin. Who knows?"

E. H. tried hard to entertain the scientificos. In the loud voice he always used when he had to force himself, he kept telling them about fishing off Cuba, hunting in Africa and fighting in the World's war. By that you could tell they were his guests, not friends, because he never entertained his friends except when he felt like it. He was more exhausted after a forced conversation with the scientificos than he would have been after a day's work, but he made them feel that he had invited them down because he liked their company and they were having a pleasant time of it. They stayed at the Ambos Mundos Hotel and were the last on board in the morning and the first to leave at night. On the way to their rooms they were shocked by the number of women who approached them on the street, and they did not try to see much of Havana.

"You ought to be nicer to Cadwalader," E. H. told me one night after they left for their hotel.

"I haven't said anything to him."

"That's just it. You might talk to him a little and make him feel welcome. He can't help it he's a stuffed shirt. He's just brought up that way. They're a funny people. They may be tough as hell in some ways but easy in others. You can't tell. We might get him to finance an expedition to Africa."

A week passed without a strike and the dark blue sea looked emptier every day.

"You have to wait for them," E. H. told Cadwalader. "Some times you might have to wait for weeks and then suddenly the sea is full of them."

"Certainly!"

"This has always been the best time. That's why I suggested that you come late in July."

"Oh, that's quite all right! You don't know what this means to me, getting out like this."

"I hope you can arrange to stay a few more days than you'd intended. I'd like to see you catch one before you leave."

"I have a round-trip ticket for ten days, but I think it can be arranged."

"Last year this time I caught seven in one day. We could have had any number of others if there had been somebody else with another rod, but I was alone with José and Carlos. You get into a run like that and there's enough for everybody."

"I gather that must have been very interesting."

"Now all the signs are right. With this northeast breeze and this current, I don't see why the hell they don't come up. Carlos said there were seven in the market yesterday."

We ran into the cove at noon, had a swim and ate lunch in our bathing trunks while we were drying off, and as we were returning to the stream Cadwalader, who was sleepy after a heavy meal, asked me to take his rod while he went below for a nap. We were trolling back toward Havana in a lumpy sea and my bait was following through a swell, down out of sight, when suddenly the rod was almost jerked out of my hands and the loose spool began spinning under my fingertips. Instead of slacking, I got excited, screwed the drag tight and struck back, pulling the smashed bait out of the fish's jaws before he had a chance to get it in his mouth.

"Why the hell didn't you . . ." E. H. began when an approaching bill thrust out of the water behind his bait and he had a smashing strike.

"*¡Córtelo!*" he shouted to Carlos and Carlos shut off the gas.

E. H. stood up between his chair and the fish box, feet wide apart, pointing the rod at the fish so the line would go out freely, with his fingertips touching lightly against the spinning spool to prevent a backlash, letting out fifty yards of line before he was ready to strike.

"*Adelante!* Ahead!" he told Carlos.

He screwed down the drag and whipped his rod back sideways three times, but the fish had dropped the bait. While E. H. reeled in, cursing softly, he had another strike and this time even when he slacked the line was alive and jerked in little bursts off the loose spool, and when he screwed the drag down and struck, the rod bent double.

A huge marlin, blue and silver, broke through a swell, raising a great white spray and leaving the spray spread out behind him as he shot clear of the water in a long forward jump. He came down tail first, plowing up more spray, and shot out again and again in two more spectacular leaps fifty yards astern, with his mouth wide open and his sword pointing toward the northwest. Then he went down, running off line while E. H. tried to get rid of Lopez Mendez's line, which had tangled around the one the marlin was on. I reeled in my bait and untangled the lines in a sort of Maypole dance, while Juan hauled in the teasers.

"The harness," E. H. said.

He was sitting in the swivel chair with the butt of the rod in the chair's socket between his legs, trying to stop the marlin with the drag screwed tight and the reel screaming, giving the bent rod and taut line as much tension as they could take without breaking, while Carlos turned the boat around on a parallel course with the fish. When E. H. had the harness on his shoulders fastened to the reel, he began working on the dragging belly of the line. With the harness on his shoulder and snaffled to the reel he could pull with his back.

Again the marlin came up through his own spray a hundred yards to starboard in six rapid splashing jumps, like a speed-boat skipping over the waves and then he disappeared, fighting deep.

E. H., with the reel half empty, tightened the drag and gripped the revolving spool with the fingers of his left hand, bearing down with every ounce of pressure he dared apply, burning his fingers on the running line until it began to slow down gradually and finally stopped. Then, with his bare feet braced against the side, with both hands gripping the rod above the reel, thumbs pressing the line against the felt, he raised the bent rod slowly and reeled a half a turn as he lowered it, then pumped hard again to prevent the fish from starting another run. The fish wanted to go to the northwest and Carlos maneuvered the boat in a semicircle ahead of the fish and turned the wheel over to Juan, who kept the boat moving forward slowly in the direction the fish wanted to go, while E. H. was pumping it up to the surface. When E. H. had the fish almost under the stern, deep down, he would say *"Poco más máquina,"* and as Juan gave the gas lever a touch and the boat moved ahead, the fish would fall back a little, coming closer to the surface, until we could see it in the wave looking as big as a submarine about to ram into the stern of the boat. Then Juan would cut down the motor and E. H. would work the fish close again, still fighting toward bottom and too deep to gaff, looking unbelievably huge and black down through the purple water.

I had the heavy Graflex in my hands, waiting for a chance to use it, and after thirty minutes of fighting, when the fish came up to the top with his fin and tail out, I took a picture and noticed it was the last one left in the film pack. When I went below to change films I heard E. H. yell "Where the hell's the Maestro?" and I knew something exciting was going on but when I got up it was over. The fish, still fresh, had made several jumps close to the stern and when Carlos leaned over and struck him in the side, the marlin broke away in a flying leap through the air and carried off the gaff in another fierce run. The gaff came loose, floating free as erect as a fence post, and two market fishermen who were standing by in their skiff picked it up and rowed it over to us while the battle continued. The marlin was still very strong and fighting hard, because, having felt the gaff, he was now afraid of the boat. He tried to sound but E. H. held him close on a short line and the forward movement of the boat kept him from getting his head down. E. H. had the cable leader out of the water six times, but was unable to raise the fish to the surface until a shark coming up from beneath struck the marlin in the flank and it came to the top in three long jumps, with the shark following, and began fighting in circles. E. H. fired several shots at the shark, driving it off, and seeing that the marlin now wanted to go with the current, he had Juan swing the boat around. The marlin made a few powerful lunges and suddenly stopped fighting and straightened out as if it had killed itself in the struggle. It came up floating like a log, belly up, was led to the stern and did not fight when it was gaffed and beaten over the head. Four of us took a hold of the handle of the big gaff and, pulling as hard as we were able, raised the marlin's head up over the stern roller, then his shoulders, getting more of him over the roller until he was almost balanced on it and then the momentum carried him forward with such a burst of speed his sword narrowly missed going through my stomach. He slammed down hard on the cockpit deck, lying on his side, a huge blue monster, round as a barrel, reaching the full length of the cockpit with his sword in the cabin door and tail almost touching the fish box. The bare hook was set firmly in the corner of his jaw. The colors, divided by a well-defined straight line running from his mouth down the middle of his body to his tail, dark blue above and silver below, began fading the instant he came on board, the vivid blue turning almost black and the silver belly darkening to the color of lead. Carlos knelt by the fish's head and kissed it with a loud smack. Lopez Mendez and the others shook hands with E. H., congratulating him, and they were all happy. I felt sad because I had failed to get pictures of the jumps.

"Cheer up, Maestro," E. H. told me. "Now you've got something to write about."

E. H., soaked with sweat after fighting an hour and fifteen minutes in the hot sun, went below for a sponge bath and a rubdown with alcohol and came up wearing dry clothes and feeling marvelous. I mixed whiskey highballs for everybody except the scientificos, who declined, and we let out the teasers and baits and continued trolling toward Havana. Henry Fowler drew a sketch of the marlin and E. H. helped him take at least twenty measurements with a steel tape. The fish was twelve feet two inches long from the end of his bill to the tip of his tail, and his girth was four feet eight inches. Carlos covered the marlin with a wet canvas and we spent the rest of the afternoon speculating on how much he weighed.

In a drizzling rain, we ran in at Casa Blanca, the small town underneath the Cabañas fortress, across the harbor from Havana, where the fishing smacks lay at anchor, side by side, and a crowd of curious natives, naked brown children and barefooted men gathered to see the fish and helped pull him on the dock. They laid him on a scale, which he tipped at 420 pounds, and, tying a rope around his tail, raised him with block and tackle and left him swinging heavily from the scaffold, head down.

E. H. sent for Dick Armstrong, the Hearst correspondent; when Dick came, he set the Graflex on a barrel and, telling everybody to be steady and chasing the kids away, began taking pictures. E. H., holding the fishing rod, stood next to the fish, his guests and crew forming a semicircle around him, and the natives crowded in from all sides in order to be in the picture. In the first one, E. H., with his glasses and cap on, was looking up toward the marlin's tail. On the next, he took his glasses and cap off and faced the camera, and then they took one of E. H. shaking hands with Sidney Franklin in front of the fish. Dick took at least twenty shots and when he ran out of film packs and had to quit we took the marlin down, loaded it across the stern and ran over to the usual anchoring place at the Havana side, where a number of Hemingway's friends were waiting to come on board.

E. H. sent me ashore for an extra quart of whiskey and when I got back the boat was full of people. Everybody we knew was on board drinking and admiring the marlin lying on the fish box, and when it became dark we turned on the cockpit dome light so they could still see the fish. It was a night of celebration. When it got late, Carlos sawed off the marlin's sword and tail for E. H. to keep as trophies, cut a few pieces for his friends, saved a slice and ten pounds of roe for the ice box and cut the rest of it into chunks small enough to row ashore and cart to the market, where he would sell it for ten cents a pound, some of the money to be used to buy cero mackerel bait and the rest to be divided equally between E. H. and the crew.

21

¡Aguja Grande!

WHEN LOPEZ MENDEZ went ashore with his cousin Enrique, Gattorno and Lillian, they invited me along for a glass of beer at the cor ner café. Enrique was feeling the effects of several whiskies, and when we sat down at one of the square, marble-topped tables, he said he was hungry.

"I should like to eat a straw hat," Enrique said.

We laughed and Enrique did not like it because we did not take him seriously.

"I mean it," he said. "I feel as hungry like a horse. I want to eat a straw hat."

The owner of the café, with the white apron tied below the bulge of his waist, brought us five bottles of beer and five empty glasses. Enrique tore the labels off the beer bottles, chewed them into small wads, moved his Adam's apple up and down and opened his mouth to prove he had swallowed them.

"Crazy! You had one too many," Lopez said.

"You see I am very hungry. I have a very good appetite for a straw hat."

"Waiter! Bring this man a straw hat. He wants to eat a straw hat," Lopez said in Spanish.

"There is none," the proprietor said, smiling uncertainly.

"I am very hungry," Enrique said, eating another label from a beer bottle.

"We serve very good meals."

"They don't stay with you," Enrique said. "I am going to eat this dish."

"No! No! ¡Loco! Stop him!" Lillian said.

Enrique put the edge of the thick plate in his mouth and, by prying the plate against his teeth, managed to break a chunk out of it, which he began to chew and acted as though he was going to swallow. Lopez Mendez jumped up and forced Enrique's mouth open as you would that of a horse you are going to bridle, and made him spit out the broken pieces of crockery.

"I think you had two too many," Lopez said, sitting down again. "Waiter, please take away these plates. It is not safe."

"I wish for a straw hat," Enrique said as the proprietor was gathering up the plates. "Waiter! Bring me corn on the cob. One cob."

The proprietor brought a cob of corn in his hand, not daring to trust Enrique with another plate. Enrique ate the corn, cob and all, and when he was finished he said he was still unsatisfied and he wanted to eat the beautiful carteras plant growing in the bucket in the corner. Lopez had to hold him down, and the proprietor, who was standing by covering his anxiety with a smile, began to look worried. Enrique ate a cigarette and two matches, swallowing them with his beer. He tore a picture of Mussolini off the wall and ate that and then he jumped up from the table when he saw a big Negro come into the café wearing a straw hat.

"Ahha! Now we eat!" he shouted, starting for the Negro with the straw hat.

Lopez caught him by the legs and held him until Gattorno got a hold of one arm and, between the two of them, they were able to handle him. Lopez knew Enrique would have taken the straw hat off the Negro's head and would have tried to eat it and there might have been a fight. Enrique kept repeating that he wanted to eat the hat and Lopez decided the only safe thing was to take him home. When they got him there, Lopez called a doctor, being afraid that his cousin might have stomach trouble, but Enrique locked his door and would not let the doctor in. He said he wanted to sleep.

The next day, they were out fishing with us again, Enrique looking as dark and handsome as ever.

"How did Mussolini's picture agree with you?" E. H. asked him.

"Poco pesado (a little heavy)," he said. "But that is nothing. One time when I get very drunk I took a plier and pulled the nail off my big toe. You can see it is only half grown on again."

"What makes you do those things?"

"I don't know. It is only when I get drunk."

The only thing we had against Enrique was that he was very bad luck. We never caught a fish of any kind any day he was on board. Enrique had some wahoo strikes on the feather and by not keeping the line taut he gave them the slack they needed to get rid of the hook, and they all got away. Nobody else could catch a fish when Enrique was on board.

Sometimes we would hear Carlos's explosive yell, *"¡Aguja! ¡Aguja!"* when he sighted a marlin's tail cutting into a wave.

"¿Dónde?" E. H. would ask, turning as he stood up and looking ahead through the cockpit windows, where Carlos pointed, while Carlos raced the motors and turned the boat around, trying to pass the baits ahead of the fish.

"¡Aguja grande! ¡Grande! (Marlin big! Big!)"

"How big?"

"Ten *arrobas.*"

"See it now?"

"No. Gone."

"Circle again."

"Gone," Carlos would repeat mournfully as we made another circle without raising the fish.

"It's good to see them on top anyway," E. H. would say, sitting down again on the tall, swiveled fishing chair. "Maybe they'll start running. It's about time. Head her further out into the current."

"What did Carlos see, may I ask?" Cadwalader would inquire.

"He saw a marlin's tail."

"A very large marlin, by any chance?"

"Two hundred and fifty pounds."

"How could he estimate the weight?"

"He could tell that by the size of his tail."

"Oh, I see."

We all tried to keep a sharp lookout for marlin but it was always E. H. or Carlos who sighted them first and pointed them out to us. Carlos saw them from the wheel if they were ahead or off to one side of the boat, traveling, and E. H. saw them first three or four waves astern when they came after the baits. I was never able to beat them at it but once, and then I wasn't sure. I was fishing Cadwalader's rod when off to the right I saw something huge and dark with light stripes like barrel hoops reflected in the sun deep in a wave. I saw it for an instant only, and then it disappeared as the hill of blue water passed.

"Marlin!" I shouted.

"Where?" E. H. asked.

"There," I said, pointing. "I saw it, but it's gone now."

"I didn't see anything."

"But it was so big I can't believe it. It was three times as big as the four-hundred pounder you caught. It was enormous."

"That's possible. Carlos, take a turn. Did you see anything?"

"No see nothing," Carlos answered.

"But I saw the stripes, even. Do you think I could have had a hallucination?"

"Sometimes you've got to see fish that aren't there before you can learn to spot them," E. H. answered. "What you want to watch for is movement."

In a good run, E. H. said we might expect to see forty fish and have ten strikes in a day's cruise. Now if we saw six marlin in a day, even if we did not have any strikes, we felt encouraged. Carlos sighted many of them from the wheel, but they would be gone before he could run up ahead of them. It was difficult to judge the exact course and speed of a fish and then to intercept it with the boat when all you had to go by might be a single glimpse of its fin or tail. When a marlin appeared in the third or fourth wave astern, a dark shadow riding with the crest and sliding down the wall of the wave, we could not be sure if it was following the baits or just happened to be traveling in the same direction. Carlos would slow down the boat enough for the fish to catch up without dropping the trolled baits, and I would run below after the Graflex, anticipating action.

If the marlin was traveling, it might continue its course without paying any attention to the baits, even though Carlos kept the boat ahead of the fish and E. H. passed the bait in front of it several times, holding his rod high and trying to tease it into striking by making the bait skip across the water like a tuna or flying fish trying to get away. If the marlin felt like playing, it might follow the baits for a mile or more, darting from one to the other without striking and then go down or turn off to one side and keep on traveling; if E. H. were able to tease it into striking, when the marlin felt the hook in its mouth it would jump straight up, dancing erect on its tail, throwing the bait twenty feet with a wag of its head and spitting out a shower of sardines and flying fish. Some of the marlin were not hungry and only struck to kill. They would attack with so much speed we could not see them turn at the end of their rushes, coming up from below or the side, sword, head and shoulders coming out as they went for the bait with their mouths open. A killer would take the bait in its jaws and go off like a torpedo, then, just as E. H. was ready to strike, it would drop the smashed bait and, when E. H. reeled in, it would strike again and drop the bait. One struck with such force it tore the two-pound cero mackerel bait in half below the hook and we could see the marks of his jaws where he had clamped down on it. It was impossible to hook those killers because they only took the bait in their beak-like jaws. What we wanted was a hungry fish that would get the bait well in his mouth, where the hook might take a hold before he started to jump.

Ward hooked a 250-pound striped marlin while E. H. was taking a nap on the starboard bunk, and when E. H. woke up he saw the fish taking off to the northwest in a beautiful succession of wild, spray-splashing, line-pulling jumps, with more than the usual excitement among the crew because the man at the rod had never had a marlin on before and they all had that desperate feeling he would lose him sure as hell. While the fish was jumping, Ward held the rod, wondering what he could do to stop the line from going out so fast. Cadwalader was reeling in his bait, Juan was pulling in the teasers, Carlos was turning the boat around to follow the fish and the first thing for me to do was to take the extra rods down to the cabin, where they would be out of the way and would not be damaged during the action in the cockpit. I raised Pauline's rod up out of its socket and the tip snapped off. I had not noticed that the hook was fastened to the roof brace instead of to the reel, and when I lifted the rod the direct downward pull of the line broke it off six inches from the end. It was Pauline's favorite rod. Nobody else ever used it and we always were very careful with it and kept it hanging from the cabin roof when she was not on board.

The fish did not go down after the first dozen jumps like the others, but kept on jumping in a straight line of spray toward the northwest, looking as small as a sardine four hundred yards away. Ward's spool was almost empty and the line was melting off so fast we knew what would happen. When the spool ran bare, the twenty-dollar line would come taut and snap at the weakest spot. E. H. screwed the drag tight and was trying to show Ward how to stop the fish when the line went slack and the fish continued jumping, making forty-seven jumps in all before he went down.

"What happened?" Ward asked.

"He threw the hook," E. H. said.

"Will he come back for it?"

"Hell, no. Reel in."

"What did I do?"

"It wasn't your fault. When you see how their mouths are made, you realize it's a bloody miracle every time you hook one."

Pauline came over to me and said, "I wouldn't feel so bad about the rod if I were you. Those things just happen. You might fish for years and never break another one. Besides, it was too long for me anyway. Carlos can fix it."

22

Thrill of a Lifetime

CADWALADER SAT with the rod in his lap day after day and never had a strike of any kind. He had found out that the closer he kept his bait to the boat, the less line there was to pull through the water and the easier it was to hold the rod. He preferred trolling with a short line because there was less friction and, as a result, he never had any strikes. The marlin, coming from astern or the side, rushed the first bait they came to, which was the one furthest astern, and the only excitement Cadwalader had was reeling his line in out of the way when the fish was hooked on the other rod.

E. H. wanted Cadwalader to catch a marlin before he went back to the States and he extended his invitation from ten days to fifteen, then twenty and finally well into August. They had been on board a month now, and it was the last day of their stay. Their boat was leaving that evening, and still Cadwalader had not had a strike. For thirty days the only thing he had felt on his rod was the dead weight of the cero mackerel plowing heavily through the waves and the jerks as it skipped out to the top, then the solid, heavy pull as it settled on the surface, trolling smoothly between Hemingway's bait and the teasers. During the past month I had never noticed any change in the expression on Cadwalader's face or in the forced joviality that he must have developed in the eastern clubrooms, where he had been taught that a sportsman is always pleased with the way things are going.

Now, on his last morning, he seemed just as eager as ever to have the sport of dragging a two-pound cero mackerel at ten miles an hour through the ocean all day, and as we were leaving the quiet, muddy water of the harbor, past the high brown wall of the Morro Castle, headed into the choppy blue of the stream, Cadwalader buckled on a butt rest, lowered a fresh bait over the side, let it fall astern, stopped it at an easy trolling distance and sat down in the chair for an all-day sit with his rod in his lap. He must have realized some satisfaction in finding out what great patience he had, I thought.

"Stream looks bloody marvelous," E. H. said.

"Oh, yes!" Cadwalader answered in a loud voice.

"Current's strong, the purple Gulf water's running close in to shore and there's a good breeze already."

"Yes, indeed!"

"Damned funny if we don't run into them today."

"I venture to say we will have a fish on board before evening."

"I'd sure like to see you catch one before you leave," E. H. said. "Damned sorry we've had such a lousy run of fish."

"Oh, that's quite perfectly all right," Cadwalader said, as if protesting an apology. "You don't know what this has meant to me, getting out here like this."

"It's a perfect day for them. If I hook anything I'll turn my rod over to you. Let out more line. See if that helps."

E. H. was unusually talkative that day because he had been entertaining these two guests a month now and he wanted to give them a good send-off. They talked about the deer and quail and prairie chickens up north and trap shooting and duck hunting in the old days. Cadwalader belonged to several gun clubs and had shot everything except big game and fished everything except big fish. He said he would like to have E. H. join his expedition to Africa and shoot a collection of gorillas and monkeys for the museum. Would E. H. consider it? Hell, yes, E. H. said, he'd shoot anything. Cadwalader wasn't positive about the expedition, though, because in the present economic crisis there was absolutely no assurance whatever.

We were trolling downstream two miles off the coast and we could see the skiffs of the market fishermen already coming in with the countercurrent alongshore, their patched sails up, bellied out from the poles at their prows. The breeze had begun blowing early and it was too rough for their small boats. The only fishermen who cared to be out in that sea were the young daredevil Chicuelo, who had won the marathon rowing championship by rowing seventy-six hours without stopping, and his brother. They were leading all the market fishermen, having brought seven marlin, three well over two hundred and fifty pounds, into the Havana market, while their father, fishing in another boat, had drifted forty-five days without a strike.

Chicuelo's skiff, now alone out in the broken blue, was riding the waves as easily as a bird sitting on the water. The sea picked it up and held it high for an instant on the top of a wave and we could see the two men balanced in the boat, Chicuelo bareheaded in the prow attending the handlines, and his brother, with the clumsy straw hat on his head and the white handkerchief over his face, sitting in the stern with the oars, rowing just enough to keep her headed into the sea. Then, as the wave rolled out from underneath her, the boat disappeared, and we could only see the two men on the water sinking into the trough and they went out of sight for a moment until they were flung up on the top of the next wave, sitting in the boat again.

"See anything over the water?" E. H. asked as we ran by.

"Nothing," Chicuelo replied, shaking his hand. "You?"

"Nothing," E. H. said.

E. H. and Chicuelo waved at each other and the skiff fell astern, floating erect and yielding easily to every movement of the sea while the *Pilar* shoved ahead, leaving a V-shaped wake and plowing spray off to each side of the bow as she cut deeply into the waves. The skiff was rising on the waves and disappearing completely in the troughs, and as we ran further away, the distance shortened the intervals when it was visible. Most of the time it was down behind the waves, which ran so high and steep I expected not to see it come up again.

"It must take guts to go out there in a boat like that," I said.

"Plenty," E. H. answered.

"You'd think any one of those waves would tip him upside down."

"It isn't so dangerous now, because he can take them head on. The danger would be in hooking a fish in this sea because he would have no control over the boat."

"Why doesn't he go in?"

"It isn't the money that makes them fish marlin, because there isn't enough in it. They do it because they like it."

"They make their living at it, don't they?"

"Sometimes, but there are a lot of damned sight easier and safer ways of making a living. Sometimes they might be out every day for two months at a stretch and not once even feel a marlin on their lines. Still they have to buy fresh bait every day. They do it because they get a kick out of it. They've got it in their blood."

"Why doesn't Chicuelo go in now? If he couldn't handle a fish anyway, why does he stay out?"

"He likes to show them he isn't afraid. He's always the last one to run in in bad weather."

"*¡Aguja! ¡Aguja!*" Carlos shouted.

"*¿Dónde?*"

"Chicuelo! *¡Aguja grande!*"

Chicuelo's boat swung around on the top of a wave and darted off toward land. Fifty yards ahead of it a 350-pound striped marlin broke water, bright silver as its wet sides glistened in the sun, shooting forward in three long jumps, exploding spray every time it came down, looking as big as the skiff it towed toward shore with the speed of a motorboat. Chicuelo was bent forward in the bow, hanging on to the sash-cord handline as the boat slanted down a trough out of sight. Without the boat, he looked like a man skiing down a hill, his brother following him as if sitting on a sled, and when they disappeared all we could see was the marlin jumping out of another hill.

"*¡Caramba!*" Carlos exclaimed.

"Christ! Now he's in for it," E. H. said. "Turn around, Carlos, we might have to pick them up."

The marlin turned and swung around in a wide circle, jumping wildly over the whitecaps, and the boat, when it rose on the next hill, had slackened its speed, was not throwing so much spray and was pivoting in the middle of that circle, which became smaller as Chicuelo in the bow hauled in the handline, pulling the boat toward the fish. The skiff kept turning with the marlin and as she went into the troughs sidewise, we expected a whitecap would break over her and sink her. It seemed a miracle every time she came up afloat. By some trick of the oars, Chicuelo's brother tilted her at exactly the correct angle to take the sea and kept her from being swamped. Chicuelo hauled the line in steadily, shortening the circles and bringing the boat and fish together so that his brother was able to gaff the marlin in the head and club it over the eyes. When the fish was dead they took it in over the side. It filled the bottom of the skiff, with its tail sticking out over the stern. Now, with their fish worth thirty dollars on board, they were out of danger, being free to take the waves head on or directly astern. Chicuelo raised the small pole to the socket built for it in the bow and let out the triangular sail made of flour sacks sewed together. The wind filled the sail and started them toward shore.

"They're real sportsmen," E. H. said. "And they don't belong to the Havana Yacht Club, either, eh, Cadwalader?"

"Brothers of mine!" Carlos said, his big teeth showing to the gums in a happy grin.

"Let out the teasers," E. H. said, and we continued trolling to eastward.

"Have you ever written any fiction about the market fishermen?" I asked.

"No."

"I should think there'd be a lot of interesting material there."

"There is. Some day I'm going to write a story about the market fishermen and it will be a good one."

"It sure must take guts to do that."

"Plenty. They've got it."

"Why do so many of them wear handkerchiefs over their faces?"

"It's to keep the sun off."

"Then why couldn't a political prisoner make his escape that way? He could come out with a market fisherman and meet a boat below Long Beach. Nobody would recognize him."

"Good going, Maestro."

"What?"

"You're getting a lot of stuff for your journalism, but it will be years before you'll be competing with me in fiction. You've got enough stuff for a magazine article now, but you don't know enough about Cuba to write a story about it. I have the advantage that I know the language. That's how I get my stuff, by talking to the people I meet in the cafeterias and hotels and other places and by reading the newspapers. If you want to be able to write fiction about Cuba, the first thing is to learn the language. You're coming along all right now. You get a word now and then and pretty soon you'll be able to put them together. Listen carefully to everything that's said and try to read the American news in the Cuban papers."

"I'm trying. How about the log?"

"All right. Get it."

I handed E. H. my rod with the feather that was fished between and far behind the two mackerel baits and he held a rod in each hand while I went for the heavy notebook with the silver pencil marking the place. I spent a few minutes every day taking his dictations in the log. It was the one thing I could do better than anybody else on board, Carlos and Juan not being able to write English. I got the logbook and pencil and sat down between E. H. and Cadwalader.

"Where did we leave off yesterday?" E. H. asked.

"Went into cove for lunch," I said, reading the last sentence in the log.

" 'Swam, talked to Rutherfords, who had lost another teaser to a marlin,' " E. H. dictated, " 'trolled back without seeing anything or having any strikes except one small barracuda Maestro caught on feather coming into the Morro.' Now today. 'On board Cadwalader, Fowler, E. H., A. S., Carlos, Juan. Four blue marlin in the market today, 11, 12, 12, 14 *arrobas*. Of these three were females and one a male. Out at 9.20. Wind east, freshening, current in close to shore, beautiful dark Gulf water within a quarter of a mile.' *¡Aguja! ¡Córtelo!"* he yelled, leaping to his feet and handing me my rod. "Slack to him! Slack to him! Don't strike until I tell you. Now strike! Strike hard. Strike again!"

A huge marlin had come up from below, its spear, head and shoulders coming clear out of the water and showing its enormous bulk as he rushed Cadwalader's bait with his mouth open and went down with it, zinging off line as Cadwalader sat with his rod whipping and line tearing off the spool, having a fish on at last and shaking with excitement. It was the biggest marlin we had seen that year. E. H. and I reeled in as fast as we were able and Juan took in the teasers. I brought Cadwalader a harness and had a hard time helping him on with it because he was shaking so much, his knees were going up and down and the rod quivered more from the movement of his hand than it did from the jerks of the fish. We were waiting for the jumps when the line went slack.

"Cabrón!!" E. H. said, swinging at the air with his fists. "Ah, *canaca! Merde!* Pfffff!"

Cadwalader said nothing. He was still shaking violently as he reeled in the limp line, which came up without the leader. The marlin, running directly away from the boat with the hook in his mouth, had reached past the fourteen-foot cable leader and cut off the double line with a slash of his tail. That meant that without his bill, he was over fourteen feet long. A fish that length could easily have weighed eight hundred pounds. E. H. would have traded the whole fishing season for such a strike from a fish that size. He would have begun his fight the same time the fish did, holding back with enough force to prevent the marlin's getting his head in a direct run, forcing him to angle off and keep his tail clear of the line.

"Now you know what a marlin is," he told Cadwalader.

Cadwalader was as exhausted as if he had fought a fish to the finish. He set his rod down and sagged lifelessly in his chair. His violent quaking subsided to a nervous tremble. He was trying to get over the shock.

"I'm damned sorry you lost him," E. H. said, feeling ten times sorrier than Cadwalader, who was still in too much of a daze to have any regrets.

"That's perfectly all right!" Cadwalader said, when he could speak. "My fault."

"You fought him very well," E. H. lied.

"Exactly what happened?"

"He cut it with his tail. He was so long he reached past the leader."

"You can't imagine what a thrill it gave me."

"I know."

"It was worth it," Cadwalader said, meaning his trip from New York and the thirty days without a strike. "Yes, sir. It was worth it."

"Now you've got an idea of what it's like to have one of those bastards on for two or three hours."

"It's a thrill of a lifetime. Yes, sir. It's a thrill of a lifetime."

"I'm damned sorry you didn't get your marlin," E. H. told Cadwalader as we were running in early to be in time for the boat.

"That's quite all right," Cadwalader said. "It was worth it. You can't imagine what it's meant to me, getting out like this."

23

Hurricane

HANK HAD BEEN stranded two months back in Key West trying to find someone to undertake the South American cruise with him in his seventeen-foot boat. He spent his time writing letters to every young fellow he knew, offering to pay all expenses, including railroad fare to Key West, but nobody could go. They were flattered to have him single them out from all his friends, they had always wanted to travel and see the world, they were very sorry to pass up this opportunity, they wanted him to know how much they appreciated the invitation and they wished him bon voyage, but they couldn't go and it was impossible to get anybody in Key West because the Conchs knew too much about boats. Hank was beginning to realize he might have to abandon his boat in Key West and with it his investment of $600 and six months' labor and give up the idea of ever selling it to a museum. He was feeling very blue when he received a reply to one of his first letters, which had been unanswered because the person he sent it to had been riding the freight trains across the country and had not been getting any mail. Bob Williams was his name. He wrote that he was sorry he had not received the letter before so that he could have sent his answer immediately. Bob said he knew Hank had found somebody else and was probably in South America with the señoritas by this time. That was just his luck, damn it to hell, when he did get a break he never found out about it until it was too late. He sure wanted to thank Hank, though, and if he ever planned any more sea voyages, Bob hoped he could get a crack at it. He'd try anything once. Hank sent Bob fifty dollars and told him to come. Bob saved the money and rode mail trains from Chicago without being caught. He was a good sort of fellow to have for a partner, and Hank made ready to leave at once in order not to give him time to think it over and back out.

They left Key West at midnight on a dark night and we watched the weather with much more interest when we knew Hank and his pal were riding the waves somewhere between Key West and Cuba. Hank had said the ninety-mile trip would take two or three days, depending on the weather, and the weather was ideal. During the next three days we had a good sailing breeze from the northeast without it getting too rough for the market fishermen. It was just what Hank needed, but he did not show up on the fourth day or the fifth and a week went by and we saw no small white sailboat come in off the blue. E. H. figured Hank had not made sufficient allowance for the current and it had carried him somewhere down the Cuban coast. His papers were made out for Havana and he would not be permitted to go ashore until he had been cleared in Havana harbor.

On the eighth day, we saw a small white sailboat working against the current about a mile off the coast; we were certain it could not be market fishermen because they always moved in close to take advantage of the countercurrent along the shore. It must be Hank, E. H. decided, and it was. He had made the trip across in three days, landing seventy miles below Havana, and had spent five days bucking the stream. The two boys in the little cockpit behind the white sail waved and yelled themselves hoarse when they saw the pointed black prow of the *Pilar* coming toward them. They were out of cigarettes, their matches had got wet and they had nothing to drink. We threw them some Cuban cigarettes and matches and tossed over a few bottles of beer, which Bob opened with his teeth. Bob looked like a good, tough kid. He was big and husky enough and had the confident, good-natured face of a fellow who has come out on top in several rough-and-tumble fights and expects a few more.

E. H. told them to move in toward shore and take advantage of the countercurrent and they made much better time that way. At sundown they were by the Morro Castle and E. H. threw them a line, towed them into the harbor behind the *Pilar,* showed them where to anchor and told them they were too late to be cleared and would have to stay on board till morning.

In the morning they were cleared and the reporters and photographers came down to interview them and take pictures of them in their boat for a page one story in the Havana newspapers, and in the evening the pretty Cuban señoritas came out in launches and asked the boys if they had any American cigarettes and invited them to come up and see them sometime. The boys found Havana very interesting. They liked it so well they never thought of leaving, and E. H. had to remind Hank that if he still planned to make his trip to South America the time to do it was now, when he had good sailing weather, because the northers would soon start and in his boat it would be impossible to head against them, they would blow him ashore. Hank put it off for two weeks and decided to leave just when there was a bad groundswell from a hurricane in the Caribbean, which, combined with a strong northeast wind, had kicked up the roughest sea in four months.

They left early in the morning while we slept, and some fishermen told us they had seen the *Hawkshaw* head straight out to sea, where it had disappeared. Even the guards on the tower of the Morro Castle had lost sight of it, and they were afraid the boys had taken a wave broadside and been buried under an avalanche of water or the wind had tipped them over.

It was the worst day of the blow and the sea was heaving up hills from the Caribbean hurricane. When we reached the top of a hill, the *Pilar* reared her prow in the air and came down with a mighty slam, slid into the trough and nosed deeply into the bottom of the next wave, with spray rearing over her and washing the salt off the cockpit windows in a blinding deluge, leaving more salt as the water ran off, clearing the windows as we rode to the top of the next one. We looked all around us every time we topped a hill, but we could see no sign of the seventeen-foot boat and we were positive we would have sighted the sail if they were still on top of the sea.

At noon we went into Cojímar, a small town three or four miles below Havana, to eat lunch, and there in the harbor we saw the *Hawkshaw* at anchor, flying the American flag and the flags of several yacht clubs. Hank and Bill were being entertained by two boatloads of young boys and señoritas that had come out to see them, and they had been invited to a fiesta in their honor at the town delegate's house that evening.

They laid at anchor three days at Cojímar, sleeping on board the *Hawkshaw* in the daytime and attending fiestas in their honor at night. When we passed the harbor on the fourth day they were gone.

24

Carlos and Juan

BY THE FOURTH of September all the guests had gone back to the States, the best part of the marlin season was over, the current was slackening off, the breeze was from the south and all the indications looked bad for fishing. E. H. decided to leave his boat in Havana and take the ferry to Key West and work on his book until the current picked up. He said he expected to be gone two weeks and that would give me enough time to write a fishing article while Carlos and Juan cleaned up the boat.

Carlos and Juan had never gotten along very well. Carlos was used to giving orders, and he figured he was now captain of the *Pilar*. What made him sore was that Juan, proud of his Spanish blood, treated him simply as an illiterate Cuban fisherman E. H. had hired to steer the boat. Juan figured, why should he take orders from Carlos? E. H. had hired him as a cook, and as long as his food was good he had done his work and it was nobody else's business if he slept during the afternoons. He was up before sunrise buying food in the market. In the forenoons he was down in the galley cooking dinner even when the sea was so rough he had to tie all the pots to the stove. In the evenings he only spent an hour or two with his woman and came back on board at nine o'clock so I could go ashore. He slept on the afterdeck bunk with the club under his pillow, ready to fight the *Terribles* if they came, and he figured he did enough. Besides, didn't he help raise the anchor every morning when leaving the harbor and every noon at the cove? Didn't he take the wheel and help whenever a fish was hooked? Hadn't he been catching scores of tiny fish in the seaweed for the scientificos? He wasn't hired to do any of these things, only to cook, but he did them by way of accommodation. What gave Carlos, an illiterate market fisherman who could neither read nor write, the idea he was captain? No, Hemingway had hired him, Juan figured, and Hemingway was the boss. Juan's reasoning was good, but Carlos did not like him personally. Juan was always showing off his education, especially when there were guests on board. He wore a yellow pencil over his ear and in the afternoons he would sit on one of the bunks with a Spanish newspaper on his knee and work Spanish crossword puzzles. If that in itself did not attract enough attention, he would spell the words out loud, growing louder and louder until we turned to see what he was doing and found him in ecstasy over the crossword puzzle. Then he would show Carlos the cartoons in the Spanish magazines and read the lines underneath. Carlos would refuse to look at the cartoons, not wanting us to know he could not read for himself, but Juan would keep on reading to him and irritating him. Carlos complained that Juan would not help him with the boat, that he was lazy and spent the afternoons sleeping up forward, that he had let the galley get dirty and full of cockroaches and that he drank too much wine on the sly. Carlos said he could get any number of men who were better cooks and would help with the boat. E. H. replied that Juan had talent for cooking, he was getting so he could handle the wheel now and he didn't want to lose any more fish this late in the season breaking in a new helmsman. Juan did his work and they would have to get along. When either of them made a complaint E. H. defended the other, and that kept them quiet. When he left for Key West, though, he told Juan and me that Carlos would act as captain and if we had any complaints we could make them to him when he came back.

The first forenoon at anchor, I stayed below at the table in the cabin with a stack of paper and a few pencils and tried to write but couldn't. I kept hearing Carlos's bare feet on the cabin roof, then Carlos singing a Cuban rumba and later on Carlos and Juan talking Spanish as they worked from the dinghy, going around the *Pilar* with a scrubbing brush and scraping off the green growth sticking to the hull just below the water line. I spent the morning staring at a blank piece of paper, trying to concentrate on an article, but my mind was muddled and I thought of everything else. I was annoyed at the interruption when I saw Juan coming down into the cabin. Then I noticed he had his hands on his stomach and was bent over and groaning with pain, saying, "Oh, my mother! Oh, my mother!" He went into the galley and poured some olive oil from the bottle into his hand and flung himself down on a bunk, completely absorbed in his pain, groaning and repeating *"¡Oi, mi madre!"* while he rubbed the olive oil over his sun-browned belly.

"Hey, Carlos!" I said. "Why don't you take Juan to the doctor?"

Carlos didn't answer because he thought it might be a trick to get out of work and leave it all to him.

"Sí, médico," Juan mumbled between his groans, that being the first time he had thought of a doctor.

"Go with him to a doctor, quick," I told Carlos.

"Then let him come," said Carlos.

Juan went as he was, without putting on his shoes or a shirt. Carlos rowed him ashore and I watched them walk up the street very slowly, Juan bent forward with his arms across his stomach. They stayed away all day and Carlos came back alone in the evening. He was excited and I could see he wanted to talk.

"How is Juan?" I asked.

"Twenty-one doctors cut him open!" Carlos said, excited by having been connected with such a big event. "Three big operations!"

"How is Juan?" I asked again.

"He was all busted inside. Three big operations. Perforated intestines, ulcers of the stomach, ruptured appendix. Three big operations at one time. Twenty-one doctors cut him open."

"How is Juan now? Will he live?"

"Who knows? It was such a big operation. But for this year he is finished for sure. No more Juan on the *Pilar.*"

"Does he get good care?"

"Like a millionaire! The best of everything! I told them he belongs to an American yacht. They think the Americano will have to pay, so they give him the best of everything. Twenty-one doctors to cut him open! If they knew he was a poor Cuban they would kick him out on the street."

"Who will pay?"

"That's for the hospital to worry about. We will fool them as long as we can. Hemingway is not responsible because Juan is only hired by the day. He did not get hurt. He was sick a long time, the doctors said. It must have been very painful to be busted like that on the inside."

"Why didn't he say something before?"

"He had fear for his job. If he said he was sick, he was afraid he would be laid off. He remembered too many days walking the streets without taking food. That's why he stood it and said nothing till his appendix busted open. I hope they do not find out at the hospital he is a Cuban!"

"Why?"

"If they do he will die for sure."

"Why?"

"Then they will know he is poor and there is nobody to pay."

"There's a hospital of the government for those who cannot pay, no?"

"Eight cents a day! That is what they allow for everything! With that they pay for sheets, food, medicine, doctors, nurses, total. The government spends forty cents a day to feed each horse of the army, but it allows only eight cents a day for the poor patients at the hospital. That is why we fear the hospital as we fear death. They die like flies in there. If your disease doesn't kill you, you starve to death. Juan is very lucky."

Carlos was proud of having fooled the people at the hospital. He had probably saved Juan's life and he was beginning to like him, now that he would not be on the boat any more.

When Carlos came back from the hospital the next day he couldn't stop laughing.

"Woman of Juan! Negress! Negress! Negress! Negress!" he said, waving his hands up and down as he bent over laughing.

I had remembered Juan telling about how good a worker his woman was and he had shown me the strong shirts and pants she had made for him when he had earned the money to buy cloth. Although he frequently mentioned his woman, he never took any of his friends home to see her and they had been wondering what she was like.

"Where did you see her?" I asked.

"At the hospital. She came to see Juan. Her face is as black as coal. Woman of Juan! Negress, Negress, Negress. Ha! Ha! Ha! Ha! No wonder he never took his friends home."

"Is she pretty?"

"Ugly. Very ugly. An old Negress. I could smell her across the room and she walks with a limp with her hind end sticking out," Carlos said, showing me how she walked. Carlos laughed easily because he was feeling very good. His enemy was completely beaten. If Juan ever got well, his crossword puzzles and his Spanish blood would mean nothing to Carlos because Carlos would always remember that he kept a black mistress, who was old and crippled and walked with her hind end sticking out.

Carlos went to the market every morning to see how many marlin had been caught. When all the signs looked their worst and after E. H. had gone home, the stream had suddenly become alive with marlin and the market fishermen reported seeing huge schools of them traveling on the surface. The motor launches had strikes all day long and broke all their tackle and the market fishermen were bringing in from twenty-five to forty a day, some weighing over nine hundred pounds. Carlos sent E. H. telegrams every night. He didn't think the run could last because there was no current and the moon wasn't right. Every morning he expected that the run had stopped, but he found the piles of fish in the market bigger than ever and the price of marlin meat down to what they had been paying for sharks. After ten days of that Carlos could not stand it any longer and he advised E. H. to come back. The morning of September 14 E. H. crossed, the breeze swung to the south and the marlin disappeared. He had missed the big run.

E. H. hired a bowlegged little Cuban named Bolo with a long narrow face and every other tooth missing to take Juan's place as cook. Bolo was the subservient sort of fisherman that Carlos wanted. He took orders from everybody with a timid *"Sí, señor,"* and helped with the work Carlos could have done alone, but he did not know how to cook and we were soon wishing Juan was back.

The last I heard, Juan was getting better and E. H. had left $200 for him with Cojo, to be paid in monthly installments so his in-laws would not be able to take it away from him. This would take care of him for a year, until he got on his feet again. E. H. never said anything to us about the money. Alphonso was the one who told me.

The stream had emptied as suddenly as the fish had come, and we trolled two weeks without a marlin strike. E. H. was disgusted after spending two months trolling in the stream every day waiting for the fish and then missing the big run completely when it did come. Now Juan was gone and chances were we would have to lose a half-a-dozen fish before Bolo could learn to handle the wheel, if we were lucky enough to have that many strikes in what was left of the season. Maybe the fish were all gone. Certainly there would not be another run such as the one we had missed, and E. H. could only stay on in hope of hooking one of the big black marlin that came after the others, just before the northers. He would have to take a chance on the boat handling.

25

Tiger Shark

THERE WERE no more guests from the States, Lopez Mendez and the Gattornos did not come as often as they had at first and E. H. and I sat alone in the stern fishing chairs for many days at a time, with no one to relieve us at the rods. There was very little talking. We would sit side by side all day long without speaking, which seemed perfectly natural, trolling, our eyes on the sea, watching the baits trail smoothly behind the jerking wooden teasers, waiting for the shadow of the marlin that did not come because they were gone.

"What do you think about?" I asked E. H. one morning.

"People," he answered.

"All the time?"

"Sometimes fish, but mostly people. You understood the scientificos. They're simple. But you should understand Juan. He's deep."

"Do you ever think about your book?"

"Not if I can help it. If I do, I try to think of something else; if I can't, that's when you may have noticed I might ask you to bring a whiskey a little early. That makes me forget and puts my mind on a different plane."

"Do you know how your book will end?"

"I do now, unfortunately. It would be better if I didn't."

"Didn't you have any idea at all in the beginning?"

"No."

I could see that E. H. didn't want to talk any more, so I laid off.

It was no use wasting gas trolling when there weren't any fish on top and E. H. decided to drift. In the morning, when the sea was flat, we ran out into the current and shut off the motor. It became very quiet and we could only hear a door squeaking and some dishes shifting in the galley as the boat rocked. Carlos put heavy lead sinkers on the leaders and we let down three baits, two from the stern and one forward, to different depths of seventy-five, a hundred, and a hundred and twenty-five fathoms. There were no fish on top and Carlos thought they might be feeding deep. While drifting, we had exactly the same chance of hooking a fish as the market fishermen had in their skiffs.

"You're sure you can tell when to strike?" E. H. asked.

"Yes," Carlos answered. He had spent forty years at this sort of fishing and spoke as an authority.

"I don't want to hook them in the guts. There's no sport in that." E. H. had once hooked a marlin that swallowed the bait and it had led to the boat in three minutes without jumping or giving any resistance whatever.

"Have no fear. We will strike before he swallows it. I can tell when the marlin takes it in his mouth."

"All right, then. I'm turning it over to you."

Carlos sat in the fishing chair with the stern rods leaning against the side, and when he became tired of holding the two lines in his hands he wrapped a line around each of his big toes, settled back in the chair and went to sleep in the sun, the lines wound in such a way that they held the ordinary pressure of the lead weight but if anything struck they would slip off and wake him up. E. H. stretched out on one of the leatherette bunks in the shade, reading a French novel, and I put on a big straw hat, found a book and went up forward to relieve Bolo so he could fix dinner. I read awhile and then drowsed off to sleep with the line in my hand. Every time the boat rocked away from the line I felt the weight of the heavy sinker, and when it rocked back the line would go slack. I woke up when I felt the line being pulled slowly through my hand and tightened my grip, but it kept going out with that same slow, heavy pull and then I knew it was more than the weight of the lead.

"Something's pulling my line!" I yelled.

"Strike!" Carlos advised.

"Now it's gone."

"You should have slacked," E. H. said. "Reel in and let's have a look at the bait."

The mackerel bait showed that a marlin's jaws had clamped it like a vise, then let go when it felt the pressure of my hand and became suspicious. It was a marlin strike, but all I had felt was the even weight added to the lead sinker and then a slow steady pull. I had not seen any huge shadow on the water darting after the baits, nor a fish come out as he took the bait in his mouth, nor felt the rod almost knocked out of my hands with the line tearing off as he went down. I had only felt that slow, heavy pull and had seen nothing. That was the difference between a marlin strike trolling on the surface and drifting deep.

It was a much easier life drifting. We would drift all forenoon with no excitement and the boat would rock us to sleep. We would wake up when Bolo had dinner ready, eat his greasy food, and go back to sleep. We could sleep most of the day on the water, sweating under a big straw hat in the hot sun, and then sleep cool all night under two woolen blankets in the harbor.

We had been sleeping peacefully for hours when a line pulled off one of Carlos's toes and he woke up with his bloodcurdling yell, *"¡Aguja! ¡Aguja!"* Half asleep, Bolo and I grabbed the two other rods and reeled in furiously, trying to get the hundred fathoms of line out of the way before the jumping began. Carlos stood holding the line over his index finger.

"Feel anything now?" E. H. asked, picking up the rod.

"Now, no."

"Gone?"

"Now he's back. I feel him taking the bait."

"Should we strike?"

"Not yet. Give him time," Carlos said, slackening line from the loose pile on the floor.

"I don't want to hook the bastard in the guts."

"I know when to strike. Slack to him."

Carlos was still saying "Slack to him. Slack to him. Let him get it well in his mouth," when we saw a small white marlin jump fifty yards ahead of the boat.

"Slack to him, hell," E. H. said and began working on the long curve of the line.

E. H. brought the fish to gaff in eight minutes. It only weighed eighty pounds, not very big or exciting, but it was a marlin and having it on board made us feel better.

The fascination of drifting deep was that you could never tell what you had on until you saw it. The first light pull on your line might be a small barracuda chopping off your bait or a wahoo or the biggest marlin in the sea.

Another time when Carlos awoke us from our dreams, we saw the line being pulled in slow, heavy jerks out of his hand.

"A big marlin!" he said. "A great big marlin! I can tell the way he pulls this is no ordinary fish. Strike him!"

E. H. took the rod and pumped and reeled, pumped and reeled as fast as he could, trying to work out the belly and have the fish on a taut line with the hook stuck solidly in his jaw before he came up to throw it in his jumps.

"A great big marlin!" Carlos kept yelling, deliriously.

Breaking the quiet peace of sleep came sudden action, with E. H. already feeling the fish, Bolo in the bow reeling in the seventy-five-fathom line and me in the stern with the other in a desperate contest to see who could get the baits on board first. E. H. had reeled in the slack and straightened out the line and now it was going back into the sea in long, heavy pulls, bending the rod double as E. H. held back with every ounce of tension the eighteen-ounce rod and two-hundred-pound test line could stand. The line loosened and he began pumping it in. Then it began going off again in a slow, steady pull that nothing could stop. What E. H. was doing with the rod and reel seemed to make no impression on the course of the fish, which took the line off as it pleased, pulling slowly for a while, then stopping, then going on again as if it were still feeding deep down.

"A gigantic marlin! A monster *grandísimo!*" Carlos yelled. He was standing at the wheel not knowing which way to turn the boat until he saw the fish jump.

E. H. saw that the fish wanted to go with the current toward shore, and he told Carlos to head the boat that way, keeping the line slanted back from the stern so that he could brace his feet on the fish box. Putting all his strength into the bend of the rod, he fought a tug of war with the fish for five minutes and then began getting line, as if the fish had become curious to see what was leading him to the surface. We were still waiting for the jumps and the suspense was at its highest pitch when E. H. caught the first flicker of yellow.

"*¡Tiburón!*" he shouted in disgust. "*Merde! Merde! Canaca!* There you see your goddamned giant marlin."

Now, having no fear of losing the fish, he horsed him in. The yellow spot showed bigger every time it flashed in the sun, and a large tiger shark came to the surface. Bolo reached the cable leader and hauled him into the stern and Carlos gaffed him in the throat. I handed E. H. the pistol, and he stood on the fish box shooting his initials into the top of the shark's head between the eyes until little jets of blood spurted up out of the holes. They were enjoying their revenge against this dirty bastard that had come to the top a shark instead of a marlin. The shark, with a clip full of bullets in his brain, was still threshing the water with his tail and snapping his teeth together when Carlos and Bolo raised his head to the top of the fish box and Carlos clubbed him over the nose. He was still swinging his tail as we raised him over the roller and let him slide onto the deck. It was the ugliest shark I had ever seen, unusually potbellied with a very wide head and a huge mouth, a backbone which protruded like that of a starved cow and a long bony tail. It weighed about five hundred pounds, stank in proportion to its size and vomited a flow of garbage over the deck. It still had a few jerks left in its tail and Carlos went to work on it again with the club. It had swallowed the bait and we had to get the hook out. Carlos got the club in his mouth and tried to pry his jaws open, but the dead shark sank his teeth into the club and Carlos had all he could do to get it back out. Carlos hit him a few more times over the nose and tried again. He pried the jaws open wide enough for a man to crawl in and let Bolo hold the club while he reached in between those long rows of pointed white teeth with the knife in his hand and cut the hook out of the shark's throat. We flung the dead shark overboard and watched him turn slow somersaults, flashing white every time his belly came up, as he sank to the bottom.

Carlos dipped up several buckets of water and sloshed the deck before the blood dried. There was a freshening breeze from the northeast and E. H. decided to troll.

26

The Whales

LOPEZ MENDEZ and Enrique were serving a spaghetti dinner they had cooked in the galley and we were all thinking about food when Carlos jumped up and let out a terrific yell.

"Cannon shot!"

"Where?"

He pointed to the northwest. "But it's impossible. It's off the target range."

"What did you see?"

"The splash of a cannon. But it's impossible. It's off the range and I heard no report of a gun."

"What did it look like?"

"Like a cannon shot, but it must have been a huge sea monster."

It came again, a geyser of spray that shot up as from a bomb bursting in the water, about two miles to the northwest.

"The devil!" Carlos said.

"Reel in. Reel in fast," E. H. said, and while we pumped up the baits he started both motors roaring and headed toward the geyser.

"No fish in the sea could make such a splash. It's the devil himself," Carlos said.

"If it is, we'll catch him."

Another spout appeared about a mile to the left of the first one.

"Whales!" E. H. yelled.

"Incredible!"

"Two whales!"

"I cannot believe it."

"Is it easier to believe in the devil?"

"But all my life have I fished in these waters and never have I seen a whale."

"Ever see the devil?"

"No, but on the sea many times have I known he was near."

"Whales are different."

The boat was going so fast we had a hard time reeling in the baits, which dragged heavily a long way astern. E. H. had her hooked up full speed, headed toward the place where he had seen the closest spout. In a few minutes we saw two spouts come up together only a few feet apart, one a tall, narrow jet of water and the other a low spray only four or five feet high, rounded like a mushroom on top, then two dark patches sliding down a wave side by side.

"Three whales!" E. H. said.

"*¡Caramba!*" said Carlos. "If we could only catch them. A whale would be worth a fortune in Havana."

"We'll try. Get the harpoon gun."

Carlos brought up Hemingway's harpoon outfit, a sawed-off, rusty, 410-gauge shotgun, blank cartridges, a dozen round sticks, some spears and coils of sash cord. This would do for harpooning mantas or turtles, but it wasn't built for whales. Instead of using the sash cord, which he knew would be worthless, E. H. fastened an eighteen-foot length of wire cable leader to the harpoon spear and tied the other end of the cable to the sixty-fathom, three-inch hurricane hawser in the bow. E. H. knew that the gun would carry the wire cable but not the rope. His effective range would only be the length of the cable, and he would have to run up on top of the whales when they came up to spout and shoot down into them. He fastened a bunch of lifebelts to the other end of the rope, so that when the whale he shot pulled off all the rope and sounded we could follow the life preservers and shoot him in the head with the Mannlicher rifle every time he came up for air until he was dead, and then it would be easy to put the big gaff into him and tow him into Havana. E. H. had it all figured out. All he needed was a good close shot and then the fun would begin.

E. H. and Bolo stood in the bow, E. H. with the harpoon gun and Bolo arranging the rope in an even coil that would run off easily. Carlos, at the wheel, was left alone in the cockpit. The rest of us were scattered over the cabin roof, Enrique holding extra harpoon sticks and the Mannlicher, Lopez with the small camera a defendant had given him when he was a member of the jury, and I with the Graflex.

The whales came on slowly against the current without any visible tail-swinging movement, seeming to lie perfectly still, drifting like logs as they came up. They stayed on top for a while, and then sank down out of sight. As we drew closer, we could see the dark shadows they made coming up, then the misty geyser spouts when they were still a few feet below the surface, then the water parting as the huge round bulks came out enough so they could breathe in air through the blowholes at the top of their heads before they went down. It was all in slow motion.

The whales did not seem to be afraid of the boat, and they let us run between them so close we could have thrown the big anchor on top of either one of them from the bow, but not quite close enough to harpoon. They were still about four feet under and we sat watching them through the clear water in the bright sun while E. H. held the gun, waiting for them to come up to the top, and Bolo stood beside him with his arms raised and his fingers tearing the hair out of his head in his excitement, shouting at E. H., "Shoot! Shoot! Mother of God, shoot!"

The huge dark bulks, slow-moving and as long and wide as the thirty-eight-foot boat, turned slightly in opposite directions as they began coming up, and E. H. waved his hand to Carlos, telling him to turn with the biggest one to the right. We were running alongside the whale when the spout came out, running straight up like a spurt from a fire hose, and then the big, blunt-nosed head with the blowhole on top came out of the water to suck in air.

"Mother of God, shoot! Shoot!" Bolo was yelling, tearing his hair out in fistfuls.

"Not close enough," E. H. said.

"Shoot! Shoot!"

"It won't reach."

"Try it, on my mother. Oh, Mother of God, shoot!"

E. H. raised the sawed-off gun, with the spear and stick protruding from the barrel, and we heard the explosion of a shotgun going off. The wire cable straightened out and stopped the spear a foot from the whale's head.

"See, I told you it wouldn't reach," E. H. said.

"Mother of God, shoot again!"

The whale reared his head and back out of the water so we had a good look at him, then his head went down in a slow turn and he sank like a sinking ship filling at one end, his tail and fluke rising in a steep slant and slipping slowly and gracefully into the sea.

Bolo pulled in the wire cable and the spear and E. H. put another blank cartridge in the gun and a harpoon stick in the barrel.

"What's the matter?" Carlos asked from the wheel.

"Not close enough," E. H. answered. "We've got to get right on top of them and shoot down into them."

"Never that one."

"No. He's spooked. Try the other. Follow directly behind and when he comes up to blow I'll give the signal and you put her full speed ahead."

"Sí, señor. Oi, caramba!"

E. H. was feeling marvelous up there in the bow with the harpoon gun while we moved at a slow trolling speed against the current, waiting for the other whale to come back up and spout. He knew by hearsay what danger we would be in if a wounded whale tried to knock the *Pilar* out of the sea, he knew what kicking power there must be in one of those gigantic flukes with a spread of twenty feet, and with all the lifebelts gone with the hurricane rope it would be a long swim three miles to shore across the slick where we saw the sharks feeding in the garbage every day. He knew there was danger and he was happy in it. This was very interesting. It was the most incredible experience he had ever had in the stream, and it would be still more incredible if he could tow a whale into Havana.

The whale's shadow darkened as it came to the top, and we followed behind its tail. When E. H. saw it was coming up to blow, he yelled *"¡Máquina! ¡Adelante derecho!"* to Carlos and as the motors roared and the boat pushed ahead, the whale veered off to the left as if frightened by the sound of the motors or the vibration of the propellers and we went on by. We tried several times to come up from the stern and the whale let us follow directly behind him but whenever Carlos sped up the motors he went down.

He stayed down for thirty minutes and we had not seen him come up again and thought we had lost him.

"There!" Bolo yelled, pointing ahead.

"There she blows!" Enrique said, pointing to starboard.

"I see one!" Lopez said, looking astern.

"Another one!" E. H. said, looking ahead.

"¡Mira!" Carlos yelled, pointing to port.

Each of us was yelling about a different whale, and when we looked around and saw what the others were pointing at, we counted six and there were more spouts coming up and it was impossible to tell exactly how many there were. E. H. said he saw twenty. Some of them were a mile or two out in the stream, the top of their spouts barely visible, there were a few astern and many ahead, not very far away, and Carlos sped the boat forward. They kept coming up and going down slowly, and there were always different whales on top.

When E. H. found out he couldn't get a close enough shot by coming up on them from the rear he tried it from the side, but the whales were so close that Carlos could not see them over the bow and he always missed them just enough to spoil a good shot. We saw three big whales a half a mile behind us, coming side by side, and the one in the middle was half again as large as the other two. E. H. told Carlos to turn the boat around and steer head on for the middle one. They had not come up to spout yet and we might still be in time for a good shot. Carlos turned her around with the motors wide open and headed her bouncing into the waves, with E. H. and Bolo standing with bent knees in the bow.

We were only a few yards away when the whales, sliding down a wave, spouted and came up for air. Carlos sighted on the middle one and put the gasoline levers down as far as they would go. We roared into a head-on collision without giving the whale time to go down, and his head was directly under the bow when E. H. lowered the gun and shot into his blowhole. Then all we saw was the rope turning off the coil and E. H. and Bolo stepping back so as not to get tangled up in it. The whale was sounding, taking off the three-inch rope like a marlin tearing line off a reel, until the spear pulled out. After that we did not get any more close shots, although we followed them all afternoon, past Havana and further on up the coast. At last it became impossible to see them in the glare of the late-afternoon sun on the water, the whales had scattered and we had lost track of them, and it was five o'clock when E. H. put the harpoon gun back into its case and we sat down to a dinner of cold spaghetti.

Nobody in Havana believed us when we said we had seen a school of sperm whales out in the stream, and that they could have seen the spouts from the waterfront. They said it was a very good story, yes, but there never had been any whales in the Gulf Stream and, naturally, we could not expect them to believe it.

27

Around Trocadero Street

A VERY PALE-FACED young man we had never seen before came
out on a launch one evening just after we had anchored. He was
a diver who had been building docks in the tropics, and he said
he had gathered material and photographs for a book on marine
life and all he had left to do now was to write it. He asked E. H.
if he thought writing it would be a good idea. He showed us his
foggy marine pictures, which he said he would depend on to put
the book over, and E. H. did not think it worthwhile to discourage
him because he would probably give it up by himself before he
finished the first chapter. The young man was pleasant company
because he was friendly and naïve and did not talk too much. He
said he was a passenger of a ship that was taking on cargo at the
dock and would not be leaving for Miami until three o'clock in
the morning. He was alone and lonesome and he wondered if I'd
care to see the sights of Havana with him.

As we started off along the dark streets toward the Prado, the
young man, who was about thirty, told me he had had gonorrhea
for three months and couldn't seem to get over it in the tropics
and that was what made his face so thin and pale. He said he
had kept the woman several months and had known all the time
that she had it, because other men had told him, and it was through
his own carelessness he had caught it. He blamed himself, not her.
I never asked him to tell me any of those things. They were interesting to him and he said them in order to give a personal touch to
our conversation. I asked him what he wanted to do downtown
and he said the first thing would be to get a piece of tail. Tail
would be higher in Miami. Now was the time to buy. He had bought
in the Havana market before. The last time he had had a good-
looking woman in the prime of her life, and he remembered her
and hoped he could find the place again. It was somewhere on Trocadero Street. She had given him her card but he had lost it. You
couldn't keep all of them and he hadn't realized till afterward that

he would remember her and want her again. He had been married since, but in five months he had never been able to get more than halfway into his wife and they had divorced. The whore on Trocadero Street was the most satisfactory woman in his life.

We found Trocadero Street down toward the waterfront, and the young man thought the place was somewhere on the other side of the Prado. As we walked along in the narrow, dark streets walled in against the narrow sidewalk by the solid front of buildings, passing barred windows and heavy doors, we could see through the windows into the lighted rooms and watch respectable-looking Cubans sitting on chairs talking to one another. I had a feeling every place we passed was a whorehouse and was always expecting to hear a woman's voice calling us, but we weren't noticed except by an old lady who clutched my arm and begged for money. We only understood that she said we were beautiful millionaires, and she, an old lady who had served the Americanos so faithfully when she was young, was now starving and all she wanted was the tip that we gave the young ones over their price. She was so ugly we broke away without giving her anything.

We crossed the bright lights of the Prado without being met by any pimps and went on into the semidarkness of Trocadero Street. All the doors looked alike, and we thought there might be women behind any one of them, but we had to be sure before we could go in. As we walked along we watched for a door that would be partly open and a young woman standing somewhere behind it whispering, "Psst! Come on, boy!"

A slender Negro girl, twelve or thirteen, no more, came up from behind us and, walking on the other side of the young man, spoke to him in New York English.

"Can I help you, sir?"

"Go along!" the young man said. "I'm fed up on 'dark meat.' Tonight I'm looking for something light."

She walked on ahead, swinging her hips and looking back at us over her shoulder.

"Come. I only work for them. I'll show you a place where you can find what you like. Twenty beauties to pick from."

We followed the dark girl because we were going in that direction anyway. She stopped at a door that was half open, pushed it into the room, showed us in and, telling the girl at the door, "Two from

Maria," so that she would get credit for us, she left us there and went back to the street to look for more customers.

"This is the place. I recognize it now," the young man said to me. *"Muy buenos notches,"* he said to the girl at the door, who took his arm and led us toward the center of the room.

"And how are you tonight, sweetheart?" the girl answered in Spanish.

"Don't understand," the young man said, shaking his head.

"I asked you how you were."

"Don't understand."

"Ah, savvy very little."

"Yes."

"But you say *'Buenos noches'* very well."

"Don't understand."

"And your friend, here, Americano too?" she smiled at me.

I shook my head and shrugged my shoulders, thinking I would get into less difficulty if I did not understand what they were saying.

"Yes. He's Americano."

"Ah!"

The women sitting on the lounges and chairs by the tables in the dimly lit waiting room got up automatically when we came in, and there was a rustling of long silk dresses and a tapping of high heels on the marble floor as they moved through the arch supported by pillars into the bright lights of the next room, where there was a big radio backed against the wall and the floor was clear for dancing, if the customers wanted to dance. We followed the women through the arch and they went over to the far corner, turned around facing us and sat down on a row of chairs against the wall. There were sixteen of them, graceful and young, none looking over twenty and really very beautiful. I was thinking none of the women in my hometown of White Earth, North Dakota could get a job in this place because they weren't good-enough looking.

"She isn't here," the young man told me. "Damn it, she isn't here. I know I'd recognize her if I saw her."

He looked across the room at the faces and figures of the young girls, trying to recognize one of them as the woman he had had there before. The girls returned our stares with different expressions, two with a fixed gaze pretending it was love at first sight, some glancing at each of us and trying to look innocent with their eyes, others with no expression at all, relying on their figures, some looking down at the floor, smiling expectantly, and the one who looked youngest really blushing. They were fresh in the beginning of the night and they sat there in silent competition, looking prettier but otherwise not much different from any other row of young women waiting for young men to come and ask them for a dance.

"No, damn it, she isn't there, and I know this is the place."

"Maybe she got the syph and they moved her out."

"No, that can't be because I had her less than a year ago."

"Maybe she's working now."

"Hell, I wish I could talk their lingo."

The young woman stood smiling at us while she listened without understanding what we said. She was wondering why we did not pick out the girls we wanted and why we were arguing, since we were not arguing with her about the price.

"He says there is one other," I said to her.

"Ah, the Americano speaks."

"Are there others?"

"No. This is all."

"He said he had one other a year ago."

"Ah, a year is such a long time, sweetheart."

"Have any gone?"

"Many. We are all new. Can he not find what he likes?"

"He remembered the other."

"Ah, he will remember us too, my love."

"He wants to find her but he doesn't know her name."

"Impossible even if he did. Our names change at every new place."

"She's gone and they say you can't trace her," I told the young man.

"I understood that much," he said.

"We have very beautiful girls, no?" the woman said.

"How much money?" the young man asked in Spanish.

"One dollar," the woman answered in English.

"I'll take that one," he said, pointing at the blondest girl in the bunch, who had light-yellow hair that was almost white and small gray eyes. She was not the best looking, but he had picked her because she was the most different from the "dark meat" he was used to. She stood up, smiling, and came over to us. The other girls shifted their eyes toward me because I was the only eligible young man left.

"I don't want any," I told the woman. "I'll wait."

"I'll pay for you," the young man offered.

"No, I'll wait."

"A buck doesn't mean anything to me. What the hell."

"It isn't that."

"Why do you not desire?" asked the woman.

"Too much syphilis."

The girls sitting on the row of chairs giggled and burst out laughing. I heard one of them say, "The Americano says he is afraid of syphilis," as if that were a comic American superstition, and there was more loud laughter.

"Well, they can't give me anything I haven't had," the young man boasted, following the blond girl to one of the rooms in the rear.

The girls got up and scattered in the waiting room, getting as much good as they could out of the soft lounges and chairs that this life provided them. They were too proud to use salesmanship and they left me alone while I waited.

When we were back on the sidewalk, headed toward the street lamps of the Prado, the young man was thinking of the girl he had just had.

"Nothing like the one I had there before, but she wasn't bad," he said. "She gave me a good workout."

"That youngest one couldn't have been over fifteen, do you think?"

"Something like that."

"She looked damned young to me."

"They mature earlier in the south."

"Yes. Especially in a whorehouse."

"Somebody's got to do it."

"Have you noticed that the women in all these places are young?"

"Of course they're young."

"What happens to them when they get old, or don't they get old?"

"Damned if I know."

All he thought about was what sort of a workout they gave him. He never thought about what happened to them after that.

We walked back to the Prado and turned up toward the theaters. We stopped under the bright lights of the first one to look at the pictures taken from the movie, but decided not to go in. When we walked away from the lights, a big man stepped out from the wall and stopped his bulk in front of us. He was tall and broad and had the slightly rounded belly that goes with a portly build. He was about thirty, wore a dark-gray suit and approached us with the dignity of a self-confident salesman who is sure of his customer.

"Good evening, gentlemen." He had learned to speak English in Boston. "Could I introduce you to some nice young girls?"

"No, we just came from there," the young man stopped to answer.

"I know some beauties. Very fine, very attractive, good, clean, young girls."

"We're not lying. We just came from there."

"Then how you would like to see a good show? You know, something hot. See them dance the cooch stark naked."

"You mean without any clothes on at all?"

"Of course."

"That ought to be good. Where is it?"

"We'd have to get a taxi. I'd have to go along to show you the place."

"How much would it cost?"

"Twenty cents apiece for the taxi. Forty cents for the tickets."

"You say they dance stark naked?"

"Of course."

"That sounds interesting. Let's go."

We got into an old Chevrolet touring car that served as a taxi, the young man and I in the back seat and the pimp in front telling the driver where to go. We drove west of the Prado and the road became so rough and full of holes the old car began rattling and shaking to pieces over the bumps and the streets became narrower and darker.

"Just so you don't take us out and hold us up," the young man said.

The pimp rested his thick arm on the cushion in back of the driver and when he turned to speak, his arm fell and hung swinging from the shoulder, because I felt his elbow bump my knee. It was so dark we could only see the shadow of his face.

"I'm on the level," he said, in a businessman's voice. "If you're afraid, I'll have him turn around and drive back."

"We're not afraid, but why the hell go so far out?"

"They can't show that stuff on the Prado. What do you think?"

"All right then, but where the hell are we going?"

"We're just about there now."

We stopped and got out in front of an old, dilapidated-looking little theater that had a light in the ticket window and a few red bulbs stuck into the concrete wall.

"Pay the driver sixty cents," the pimp said.

"I thought you said twenty cents apiece."

"Right, and there are three of us. Do you think he'd let me ride for nothing?"

The young man paid.

"He'll wait if you want him to take us back downtown. It might be hard to find another taxi here."

"All right. Tell him to wait."

The pimp went ahead of us to the ticket window and spoke Spanish through the hole to the man sitting behind the glass.

"Cuarenta centavos," he said. "That will be one dollar and twenty cents."

"But it says ten and twenty," the young man observed.

"That's for balcony seats only. You want to get up in front where you can see it."

"Do I pay for you, too?"

"Do you want me to wait outside?"

"No, but . . ."

"If you want me to go and leave you here, just say so. I'm trying to show you fellows a good time, but if you don't appreciate it, I'll go."

The young man paid a dollar and twenty cents for three tickets, which he dropped into the glass box as we went into the dark theater. We walked on the cement floor down the aisle, past scattered groups of smokers and children, toward the lighted stage where two young men, the short one wearing pants that were much too big for him and the tall, slim one in a suit that fit as tight as underwear, were slapping each other and trying to be funny in Spanish. You did not have to understand the language to know it was lousy comedy. We went up in front near the stage to one of the heavy planks which sagged in the middle and bounced like a springboard when we sat down on it.

"When are they going to do the cooch?" the young man asked, in a pleasant humor.

"Pretty soon. Pardon me for one moment, please." The pimp left us to get his cut on the tickets at the office and when he returned he was smoking a cigar. "Well, gentlemen, how's she going?"

"We haven't seen any cooch yet."

"They can't play the same number all the time. This vaudeville is good."

"But we can't understand it."

"It's hot stuff. Ha, ha, ha, ha!"

A woman in a blue evening gown came out and the men stood in the rear wisecracking as she walked back and forth in front of them, rocking her hips.

"We don't get any kick out of this."

"He's telling her to kiss his rectum," the pimp lied.

"You know, this might be good if we could understand it," the young man said to me.

I didn't tell him it was lousy because he had paid for the tickets. The pimp entertained us for a while by translating dirty remarks that he invented himself as the vaudeville went along, but after a while the young man got tired of it.

"Lookit here," he said. "We came out here to see a cooch. We paid to see a cooch and now where is it?"

"She'll be out soon. She's got to have some rest. You can't expect her to do it all the time. There she is now."

The same woman in the tight-fitting blue evening gown came out again. She walked past the tin-covered footlights with her hands resting on her rolling hips and her skirt trailing behind her heels.

"Hell, do you call that the cooch?"

"Give her a chance."

A piano began to tinkle some Cuban music and the woman sailed across the stage, mixing short steps with some long graceful sweeps, holding the bottom of her skirt up in her hand, and when she circled on her toes, her dress opened and raised like an umbrella and we could see her bare legs. She took off her dress piece by piece while she was dancing, and when all she had left on were a few long strings of beads and a grass skirt the men in the audience began shouting. The music was going faster, and instead of the long sweeps she had taken at first with her dress, she was now rolling and pumping her hips and shaking herself like a dog when he gets out of water. When she left the stage, she still had her grass skirt on.

"Hell, I thought you said she'd do the cooch stark naked," the young man said. If she had taken off the grass he would have been satisfied that he had got his money's worth, but as it was he had seen nothing more than he could see at any burlesque show in the United States and he felt that he had been gypped.

"What more can you expect?" the pimp asked. "Wasn't that hot stuff?"

"You said she wouldn't have any clothes on."

"You can't expect the girl to stand up there and show her bare rectum for forty cents."

"Well, that's what you said. That's why we came out here."

"I'm sorry, gentlemen. If you are not satisfied, I'll pay you your money back out of my own pocket, but what can I do? I meet you downtown, I never see you before, you ask me to take you to a hot show and what can I do? If I had taken you to see that kind of stuff, how do I know you would not get offended? You see how it is?"

"You say you can take us where we can see it?"

"Certainly, gentlemen, but it would cost you more money."

"How much?"

"For fifteen dollars you can see anything you want to see."

"To hell with it."

"It's all right, gentlemen."

"Let's get the hell out of here," the young man said, disgusted.

"It's all right, gentlemen. Anything you say."

On our way back, the pimp said he knew all the girls in town and he wanted to introduce us to some of them and show us around to the different places and it would cost us not a cent unless we felt like spending money. We got out downtown and went into many elegant places and priced many beautiful señoritas in silk evening dresses, but always found them too high or not exactly what the young man wanted and left without spending any money. The young man knew he would take one on after a while, but he was in no hurry this time, it would be better the longer he waited. After working several months in the jungles, he was glad to be back to civilization and was enjoying this stroll from place to place. Some of the matrons asked five dollars and he knew it was a holdup because he was an American. The English-speaking matrons said their girls were all medically examined every week and guaranteed to be pure and if you wanted wholesome stuff, you had to pay for it and they told him how diseased he would get if he went to the cheaper and less reliable shops. The young man insisted they were all holdups, and the pimp admitted the rates were higher for the Americans because the Americans were more likely to get drunk and beat the women and break the furniture and they had to charge them more to make up for it. He took us to some less expensive places where the rent and upkeep weren't so high, and in one of them the young man was astonished to find the very woman he had been looking for. She was a big-breasted, muscular blonde with hard, slender legs and when she walked lazily over to us he could see she did not remember him.

"See anything here you like?" the pimp asked.

The young man was flushed and embarrassed when he first saw the woman he had remembered and thought about for several months and here she didn't even recognize him. She came over to us, raising her eyebrows questioningly as if we were new customers and she had never seen us before.

"I'll take her," the young man said, without asking her price.

The woman nodded and led him into another room.

Much sooner than we had expected, the young man came back out, tightening the knot of his necktie, with a disgusted look on his face.

"What's the matter?" the pimp asked.

"When I had my pants and shirt off, she asked for a dollar and a half. A dollar was all I paid her before."

The woman had added fifty cents to pay the pimp as his commission.

"What did you tell her?"

"I couldn't talk enough to tell her anything. I just put my pants back on. To hell with her."

"Maybe she'll come down."

"No. To hell with her. If you can't find us a dollar place, we'll go back to Trocadero."

The pimp took us to another door on the same street and after a long argument and much headshaking, the matron finally fixed the price at a dollar and the young man went off with a big-mouthed brunette who had wide, open spaces between her short teeth. While we waited, we sat down near the matron, who was plump and middle-aged with a kind, motherly face. She was sitting at the open door watching the pedestrians and saying "Pssst," whenever any men walked by.

"Does he understand Spanish?" she asked the pimp about me.

"A little," he answered.

"How many years have you?" she asked me.

"Twenty-two."

"So young! Just a baby!"

She heard people coming on the sidewalk and she had to turn her face to the street. She said "Pssst!" as three young men passed the open door without turning their heads.

"I suppose he thinks it's shocking to see me call to the people on the street."

"Oh, no. It's business," I said.

"You understand what I said?"

"Yes."

"You're just a baby."

"But the girls—they're my age, but you wouldn't call them babies."

"No, they've seen more of life."

"Do you have much to do with the girls?" I asked the pimp.

"No!" he said, insulted. "What the hell! I'm married. I got a wife and two kids."

It was past midnight when the young man said he wanted to go back to his boat so as to be sure not to have it go off and leave him. The pimp wanted two dollars for having shown us around all night and they argued in loud voices in the quiet, dark street. The young man gave the pimp seventy-five cents to get rid of him, and they parted equally disgusted with each other.

28

Goodbye to Havana

THE CUBAN COAST looked as dark green and fresh as it had in the spring when we came over, but we could tell it was fall by the tang of autumn in the air, which had become cooler and windier. The offshore winds blew small rainclouds off the land in the afternoons, and the sudden squalls kept the hills fresh and green and we could smell the hills way out in the stream, but when the wind swung to the north it was a cool, dry wind with winter behind it and we were reminded that the season was almost over. The stream seemed to be emptier every day, and we did not have much to look forward to except the possibility of hooking into a big marlin and seeing it make the same kind of jumps, the difference being it might put up a stronger fight and would weigh more on the dock and look bigger in the pictures. Soon the northers would begin to blow, and before they came we would have to go back to Key West. It would not be long now and we were all thinking about it. The worthwhile part of the marlin season had been over a long time, all the other motor launches had given it up a month ago, there were not many market fishermen to be seen in their skiffs and we were alone every day in the stream except for the big ships passing in and out of Havana. No guests came with us and we no longer went into the cove to swim and eat, but had our lunch out in the stream, drifting when it was calm and trolling through an empty sea when it was too rough to drift. There was no more of the spirited conversation there had been in the beginning with the Gattornos and Lopez Mendez. Now, alone, we talked less every day as we were coming to the close of a disastrous fishing season, having taken only twelve marlin in three months. E. H. knew it was not much use staying on, but he wanted to fish the season completely through to the finish and could not make up his mind to leave. Carlos and Bolo were very sorry the season was almost over and they would lose their jobs without having saved any money to eat on. Carlos, from his experience with E. H. in other years, told me he expected to get a $200 tip on top of his wages, but Bolo had only been with us a few weeks, he knew he had not been good for much and he could not expect more than he had coming. He wished he was me, he said, so he could go along and stay on the boat at Key West. I had been very eager to come over, I had had a wonderful time in Cuba, but now returning to Key West would be something different again, going back to that quiet, restful life of fishing half days. Although not as excited about it, I was almost as eager to go back.

We had fished in silence all day, drifting in the morning and trolling in the afternoon when the wind came up, and toward sunset, as we were coming in, E. H. hooked a 400-pound striped marlin that came out in a beautiful succession of long, greyhound leaps and Carlos, swinging the boat around with the motors wide open, raced alongside on a parallel course with the fish.

"Not so fast," E. H. said, working on the long U of the line.

Marlin meat being worth ten cents a pound in the market, Carlos was seeing forty dollars coming out of the sea with every jump, and he kept the motors at top speed, racing with the fish as if trying to head it off.

"*¡Córtelo! ¡No tanta máquina!*" E. H. yelled, with his bent rod pointing astern, while the fish was jumping ahead to the right.

"*Sin juventud* [without youth]," Carlos replied, too excited to take orders.

The fish broke off and E. H. reeled in the empty line. He told Carlos that too much speed in chasing a fish was the worst thing they could have, that it put so much strain on the belly of the line it was impossible to avoid breaking off the fish, chasing it that way, but Carlos answered that he had been fishing marlin forty years and he could not believe he had done wrong or lost the fish through lousy boat handling.

On October 15, E. H. cut his left index finger on the fin of a small blue runner he had caught drifting; it was only a surface scratch and he never noticed it until a few days later, when it started an infection and the finger swelled to twice its normal size. Then his whole fist swelled so that it was smooth across the knuckles with red streaks spreading up along the veins of his arm. E. H. had the finger lanced and bandaged and went fishing every day, even though the doctor was uncertain whether it would turn into blood poisoning and advised him to stay in bed and keep his hand in hot water and Epsom salts. E. H. was always the first to insist on having a doctor and following his orders if anything happened to any of us, but with himself it was different. He ignored the torture as if he never felt it. I could see the pain in the hardened expression of his face, but he never complained and something told me not to ask him how his finger was when he came on board in the mornings, although he had always asked me how I felt when I had a bad knee.

The swollen hand and the spreading red streaks on his arm looked more like blood poisoning every day, without being aggravated. I knew E. H. would fight anything that grabbed his hook and I was afraid he would kill himself on a big fish, but, fortunately, he did not have any strikes and one morning the first bad norther was kicking up such a big sea, blowing the white caps off the crests of the waves, there was danger of losing the ship and we had to turn back into the harbor. E. H., realizing there was no fishing weather left except between the northers, ran the *Pilar* over to Casa Blanca, had her put on the ways, her bottom scraped and painted, and when he slid her back into the water and filled the gasoline tanks a few days later we were ready to leave.

They were all down to see us off the last night. All the people in Havana who had fished with us during the summer came on board, and the cockpit was the fullest it had ever been and I could scarcely get through with the whiskies. They were all there, comic Lopez Mendez, still wanting to marry an American girl, Ginger Rogers preferred; his dark, silent cousin Enrique, the straw-hat eater; the great artist Gattorno with the weak voice and delicate face and his beautiful wife still keeping him broke smoking American cigarettes at eighty cents a pack in Cuba and believing she would become a movie star automatically when she arrived in Hollywood; there was Julio, the big, hoarse-voiced pilot, who swung his arms dangerously when he talked; Cojo, the goodhearted mechanic who loved to sit and listen; Dick Armstrong, the Havana newspaper correspondent who always came out to the dock at Casa Blanca and took pictures for us when E. H. had a big marlin strung up; Aliende, the half-starved purchasing agent, who was delivering a huge antique vase E. H. was taking over for Pauline to have in the yard in Key West; and the Gallego, the wine-drinking chauffeur, who always used to ask, "You have *vino para me?*" They were all talking, so there was no connected conversation, and they were all drinking just the right amount of whiskey to feel good, under the dome light of the cockpit roof.

We had to leave before midnight because the clearance papers were made out for that day, the eighteenth of October, but E. H. was waiting till late as the sea was smoothest between midnight and morning. At five minutes to twelve the guests said goodbye, shaking hands with E. H. and wishing him luck as they piled into the skiff that carried them over to the black pilot boat, and E. H., Carlos and I were left alone.

I went forward to help Carlos lift the big anchor out of the mud and E. H. started the motors and headed the *Pilar* into the dark, open gap between the tower of the Morro Castle and the lights of the Havana waterfront. The black pilot boat, with Hemingway's friends still feeling the effects of the whiskies I had mixed, followed us out of the harbor, past the stone wall of the tower into the open, dark sea.

"Goodbye!" they yelled in a chorus and we could hear Lillian Gattorno's shrill voice above the others.

"Goodbye!" E. H. answered, Carlos and I listening.

"Farewell!"

"Farewell!"

There was an interval of silence while we watched the running lights of the black ship scarcely visible beside us and then they started up again with their goodbyes and farewells. They followed us about three miles out and then we saw the red running light turn around and change to a green one as we saw the other side of the boat headed back to Havana.

It still blew from the northeast and when our eyes got used to the dark we could see the whitecaps of the waves in the dim star-light. The *Pilar* headed north, cutting sidewise into the running waves, both motors hooked up, and sometimes she rolled so much we heard the side propeller thrump when it came out of the water. Only the binnacle light was on, and Carlos sat at the wheel steering and looking down into the compass. I knew he could not read and I did not believe he knew anything about steering a boat in the dark by a compass, but E. H. trusted him and I wasn't afraid. E. H. lay on the starboard bunk with a blanket over him and went to sleep, so that he would be fresh to take the wheel when Carlos became sleepy. I looked down over the stern with the flashlight every once in a while to see if the water pumps were pumping, and when I saw the water spurt out of both holes I sat back in the fishing chair and watched the row of lights of the Havana water-front growing smaller and shorter, the lights coming closer and closer together. I sat watching and waiting for them to join into a solid white line, so that I could not distinguish any one of them, and they were almost but not quite touching when they dipped under the last wave.

Simple Words Are the Best

BACK IN KEY WEST, the island seemed very small; the life was much easier after the strain of fishing every day, all day in all weather off Cuba. Now there was plenty of time for everything. We only went out in good weather half days and, after the marlin, catching sailfish and dolphin was more like play than a sport. E. H. had no more need of discipline and I became his boatman and a member of his family again, and he treated me like a father treats a son he is training and trying to make something out of. While finishing his book *Green Hills of Africa,* he was in the genial humor of a writer who is doing good work and knows it, and he didn't seem to mind my continuous questions about writing when he came down to the boat or I went up to his house.

"Do you think I'll ever make a writer?" I asked him.

"You're getting better. Much better. If you have talent, it will show up later."

"Do you think I have talent?"

"Nobody can tell that. You have to give it a chance to develop."

"If I don't make a writer, I suppose I could get a job on a newspaper."

"That isn't the way you want to figure. You want to make up your mind to do it if it kills you."

"I was thinking about a few years from now if I find out for sure I don't have any talent."

"Keep on working and don't get so discouraged. You're the most easily discouraged person I know. That might be a sign of genius but you've got to get over it. Forget about newspaper work. Do anything else to make a living, but not that. Newspaper work is the antithesis of writing and it keeps writers pooped out so they can't write; besides, there's no future in it. The only ones who can possibly do newspaper work and write are supermen who have such brilliant minds the newspaper work isn't anything at all for them, but you're not that type. You've got to have time and you never would have made a fast newspaper man. The most fortunate thing that ever happened to you is that the editor of the Minneapolis *Tribune* refused to give you a job."

"But you used to be a newspaper man and you became a writer."

"In spite of it."

"You know that story you wrote about Cuba? The natives here all tell me it actually did happen."

"If it were true, they could put me in jail for it. That's the business of literature, to make them believe it."

"I'd like to try to write some fiction."

"You're not ready for that yet, but go ahead and try. Don't write any fiction about Cuba, though, because you don't know enough about it. It would be easy for you to make up some exciting adventures in Havana and they would seem good to you, but that would be because you don't know enough about the country to know whether they're good or not. What is hard is to write about something you know about and know thoroughly, because then when you read your stuff over you can tell if it's bad."

"Is it best to live in the place you're writing about?"

"Never write about a place until you're away from it, because that gives you perspective. Immediately after you've seen something you can give a photographic description of it and make it accurate. That's good practice, but it isn't creative writing."

"In fiction, if you invent as you go along, how do you decide what will happen?"

"Out of a dozen interesting possibilities you pick the inevitable."

"How can you tell if it's bad?"

"Something inside you tells you that. If it's on the borderline, you might have to show it to someone else, but you can usually tell."

"You know, I think my first trouble was that I tried to stick in too many fancy words."

"That's the trouble with so many. Big-time writing never changes. Pick your vocabulary from the words you hear people speak in conversation. They've stood the test of centuries. The simple words are always the best."

"Whenever I try to write, it always seems like I want to be doing something on the boat."

"Sure, that's because it's a hell of a lot easier than writing. That explains why I followed bullfighting and a lot of other things I've done."

"Does it explain the marlin expedition?"

"Partly."

"And fishing now in the afternoons?"

"Fishing is a sure way to rest the mind."

"Damn, I wish I could write. I'm trying, but it's so hard."

"Sure it's tough, and you're just beginning to find that out. The better you write the harder it gets. What you want to do is practice a little every day. You ought to be able to write at least two hundred and fifty words a day and that's plenty. That would make two novels a year. The important part is to keep using your eyes and ears. Watch all the people you see on the dock, when the yachts come in watch the owners and the men on the crew, watch every move they make and see how they're different, listen to everything they say so you can remember every word and how they said it. You're sensitive yourself, and that's one thing you've got to be, but you've got to be sensitive to other people too. You've got to be able to feel as they feel and know how they think. If you keep trying, you can develop that. Nobody's interested in what you suffer. If you just wrote about your own sufferings, you'd just be a goddamned bore. Who you are or what you are or what happens to you doesn't make a damned bit of difference to anybody. Forget about yourself and try to look into other people's heads and see how their minds work."

"If I can't write fiction about Cuba, what should I write about?"

"It isn't that I'm trying to keep you out of my racket. You simply don't understand it well enough for fiction. In fiction, it's what you can leave out that counts. Nine tenths of it has got to be beneath the surface. That's what gives dignity to a story. The thing for you to do now is to write some fishing articles about Cuba. You should be able to fix up something they'll take and you can have all the pictures I've got. Write your journalism first, it's good practice putting it down on paper as it actually happened so the reader sees it and gets the emotion. Then when you start with your fiction afterward, write about something you know real well. You ought to have plenty stuff about bumming."

"That's the way it seems to me. You know, I can't remember anything interesting about the four years I spent at the university. All that seems an empty blank, and everything that I've seen and has happened to me was afterward on the road or before, when I was a kid."

"That's because when you're young you're more sensitive. That's when everything impresses you most. Most writers keep on writing about their childhood until they're forty. They spend their youths concealing their love affairs and their old age revealing them. The best stuff you've got is from your farm life in North Dakota and your sister's murder. That's something nobody else can write and nobody can ever take it away from you, but you don't want to use it for a long time. Save your best stuff until you've learned how to handle it, because you can't write the same thing twice unless you rewrite it. Wait until you've learned how to become detached. In order to write tragedy you've got to be absolutely detached, no matter how much it hurts you. Tragedy is the peak of the art and that's the hardest thing there is to do. You never lose a story by not writing it."

I wrote a piece about fishing and E. H. was happy to see an improvement in my work. He said there were awkward places but he did not bother to point them out or change the wording, because he said that was not very important, as it would work itself out in time, but he checked the inaccuracies and showed me parts of the action I had left out and told me what to put in to make it complete. I was very happy when he had gone over it and figured it was as good as sold, but when *Field and Stream* promptly sent it back with the usual rejection slip I was down in the mouth again. In order to cheer me up, E. H. offered me a bet of seventy-five dollars against twenty-five that if I sent it to *Motor Boating* they would take it. He won the bet but refused payment. When I showed him the February issue, with the happy feeling a writer always has when he sees his words printed on smooth white paper the first time, E. H. seemed to be even happier than I was.

"Well, Maestro," he said. "Now you are a writer. Why don't you stick around and go with us to Bimini next summer? You might get something for the *Saturday Evening Post.*"

I did not answer because I knew I would not go again. I had had a good time in Cuba but I was not a fisherman at heart and, having been cooped up on the *Pilar* for almost a year, it was time to move on to a freer, more natural life and get my own stuff and see what I could do with it. The Key West naval yard was changed to the city yacht basin, and three shifts of WPA watchmen were

employed to be responsible for the boats, so it was no longer necessary to have anyone sleep on the *Pilar*. I told E. H. I wanted to
go home and see the folks.

"I know," he said. "It'll make them feel better and now that
you've sold your first piece, you can show them something you've
done. But, whatever you do, you'd be foolish if you don't make
use of the rest of the stuff you got in Cuba. You've used the easiest
stuff now, but there should be plenty left. I'd been planning to
help you along with it, but you're getting so you can write journalism
now and you might be able to do it by yourself. I'd been hoping
that you'd get going good with your stuff so that when you left
you'd have a trade."

The last morning I put away the blankets, locked the boat, pulled
her off and took my knapsack up to the house. I found E. H. in
the hallway handling varnished marlin spears hung on the wall
and he told me to come up to his workshop. He had some things
to tell me before I left and he sat down behind his desk, as he
had at our first interview, and began to speak seriously.

"The main thing you've got to overcome is getting discouraged,"
he said. "You have physical courage, but then everyone has until
he's been scared. What you need to develop is moral courage and
that's much more difficult. For Christ's sake, don't get discouraged!
Writing prose is the hardest thing in the world. There are only a
dozen great writers alive, and you can't expect to write anything
fit to print in a year. If you do it'll just be an accident. I tell you
frankly you're just as far behind in writing fiction now as you were
in journalism when you first came here. For Christ's sake, don't
get discouraged! Work hard and know when to stop. You'll find
there are times for weeks at a stretch when you can't write, and
when that happens don't get discouraged. Every writer has times
when he can't write. It's natural. It's to be expected. When you
run out of juice, write accurately the things you see so that they
become alive on paper and you make the reader see them. Notice
not what people should say but exactly what they do say, how they
say it, the inflection of their voices, how they look, their distinguish-
ing features. Those are the things that make writing alive and
you want to practice writing them so that you give the reader the
exact picture and then try to figure out what gives you the emotion
so that you can make the reader feel that, too. That's the way I
learned how to write.

"Your articles have been good training for your eyes and describing things as they actually are has given you a true slant on writing. Now, when you go up north on this trip you might get an idea for a story and you'll see more than you did in all your previous bumming. Then when you get home, when you can't write fiction, go out and see something and make it alive on paper. Talk to people and write what they say exactly as they said it, then your mind automatically begins to listen for conversation, you develop a good ear and your minds acts as a sieve so you forget what you can't use. You want to read good stuff and develop good taste and none of it will be time wasted.

"Don't start sending anything off until you're damned sure you're writing good stuff. When you've got some good stuff, come down here with it and I'll always be glad to go over it and tell you what's wrong with it. Whether it's six months from now or a year or two years, we'll always be able to fix you up with a place to sleep.

"But for Christ's sake don't get discouraged and don't worry about it. Never worry about your writing because that poops you out and makes you impotent. Get plenty of exercise and keep healthy. That's the main thing."

We went down to say goodbye to Pauline and when I went through the iron gate they waved, standing together by one of the palm trees beside the house. I waved back and I felt a sore lump in my throat growing bigger as I struck off on Duval Street toward the highway.

"E. H.: A Coda from the Maestro"

(Arnold Gingrich's "Publisher's Page" from *Esquire*, October 1961)

ERNEST HEMINGWAY, as he wrote of Ring Lardner in these pages in September of 1934, "has not been dead long enough for anyone more interested in literature than in the personality of his friends to criticize him with the impartial scalpel of the post-mortem examiner."

He was, as we duly reported on a number of occasions, one of the best friends this magazine ever had, and that at a time when its need of friends was the greatest. It is not too much to say that, at the very earliest point, he was its principal asset. We are referring, of course, to the very beginning. We had Hemingway for a start, and with his knowledge and blessing, used the fact that we had him as a talking point to enlist others. We were going around New York with a checkbook, calling on writers and artists all and sundry, trying to make them believe that we were actually going to come out with a luxury magazine, "devoted to the art of living and the new leisure," at the very moment when the banks had just reopened, and people were still only hoping that the Depression was about to end.

We'd take out the checkbook and write the prospective contributor a check, and depression or no depression, the response was always mixed. First, pleased surprise at the sight of some money, and then, as an invariable double take, "But you aren't getting Ernest Hemingway for *that*, are you?" Then we had to say no, that our gentlemen's agreement with Hemingway was that we would pay him twice as much as we paid anybody else, and that, while we hoped to pay more, if and as the magazine succeeded, we were still honorbound to preserve that ratio. Such was the stature of the man that even then (Spring of '33), nobody objected.

But this isn't going to turn into one more of those ubiquitous Farewells that have flooded the public prints since the second day of last July. We made our separate peace with him, long ago and in these pages, and his death is no excuse to begin wallowing in anecdotage now.

But we do feel impelled to pass on a few random recollections from his writings, still uncollected for the most part, that appeared regularly in this magazine throughout its first three years. They are scattered sentences that we had occasion to remember when we learned the manner, as well as the fact, of his passing.

First, as if flashed on a screen, we recalled a passage in *A Paris Letter,* that we looked up and found in the issue for February, 1934:

> It is very gloomy. This old friend shot himself. That old friend took an overdose of something. . . . People must be expected to kill themselves when they lose their money, I suppose, and drunkards get bad livers, and legendary people usually end by writing their memoirs.

From *Notes on Dangerous Game,* in July, '34, we remembered:

Any good man would rather take chances any day with his life than with his livelihood and that is the main point about professionals that amateurs seem never to appreciate.

But most of all, we twinged at the recollection of "Monologue to the Maestro," from the issue for October, '35. The Maestro, mentioned often in the letters from Key West and Cuba, was a boy from Minnesota who wanted to learn to write, who hitchhiked down to Key West and was taken on as a sort of apprentice hand on the boat. He was called the Maestro because he played the violin. He had a lot of stories he wanted to tell, and Hemingway was going to try to teach him how to tell them.

Maestro: Do you think I will be a writer?
Your Correspondent: How the hell should I know? Maybe you have no talent. Maybe you can't feel for other people. You've got some good stories if you can write them.
M.: How can I tell?
Y. C.: Write. If you work at it five years and you find you're no good you can just as well shoot yourself then as now.
M.: I wouldn't shoot myself.
Y. C.: Come around then and I'll shoot you.
M.: Thanks.

We'll let the Maestro end this. His name is Arnold Samuelson and we heard from him, right after the event, from Texas.

"Ernest lived as long as he could. His last act was the most deliberate of his life. He had never written about his own suffering. He said it all without words in the language any man can understand."

—A.G.

About the Author

ARNOLD SAMUELSON was born in 1912 in a sod house in North Dakota. He wanted to be a writer all his life; he majored in journalism at the University of Minnesota (although he never officially graduated because he wouldn't pay the $5 diploma fee), and became a cub reporter on the Minneapolis *Tribune*.

After his sojourn in Key West, he published articles, married, broke wild broncs for ranchers, and worked near the Arctic Circle during World War II. After the war, he moved to Texas and had two children, Eric and Diane (she discovered and edited this manuscript). He died in 1981.